FOOTPRINTS OF JESUS

Part 2

Footprints of Jesus

PART II

MIRACLES AND MINISTRY

By W. L. Emmerson

Author of "Bible Certainties," "The Bible Speaks," "God's Good News," etc.

ILLUSTRATED WITH MASTERPIECES OF
SACRED ART AND SCENES FROM
THE HOLY LAND

THE STANBOROUGH PRESS LTD., WATFORD, HERTS.

CONTENTS

ACKNOWLEDGMENTS

OUR grateful acknowledgments are due to the following for permission to reproduce their copyright pictures: CAMERA CLIX, front endsheet, pages 12 40 52 84 96 104 120 160 168 176 180; JOHN H. EGGERS and the BROOKLYN MUSEUM, pages 80 108 140 148 156; EYRE & SPOTTISWOODE, page 39; W. E. FILMER, pages 25 76 101; HANFSTAENGL, pages 28 44 88 135; S. H. HORN, pages 133 144 145 172; LAMBERT, page 107; T. NELSON & SONS; pages 36 68 112 124 152; NEWTON & CO., page 184; PALESTINE EXPLORATION FUND, rear endsheet; RELIGIOUS NEWS SERVICE, page 27; STUDIO LISA, page 67; THREE LIONS, pages 8 16 24 25 64 65 100 132 136 173; C. D. WATSON, pages 101 133 144 164 165.

Illustrations

BIBLE PICTURES (In Colour)

SCENES IN BIBLE LANDS (In Colour)

MONOCHROME ILLUSTRATIONS

still appearing pious, the Jews devised endless formulæ which sounded like oaths but did not bind them in any way. To swear by heaven or earth, for example, was not as binding as to swear by the character of God. But such subtleties, Jesus utterly repudiated for, He said, heaven is "God's throne" and the earth is "His footstool." To swear "by Jerusalem" likewise absolves no-one for it is "the city of the great King," and even to swear "by thy head" is to involve a part of the creation of God.

Apart from the wholly proper oaths, said Jesus, a promise needs no more than a "yea, yea" or a "nay, nay" where there is honest intent to perform. Any tortuous attempt at evasion "cometh of evil."

So in His discourse on the law of God, Jesus not only cleared Himself completely of the accusation that He had come to destroy it, but He turned the tables upon His accusers, revealing how fearfully they had perverted it and how valueless was the righteousness which they were at such pains to establish.

This indictment of the Pharisees of Jesus' day has a dual relevance in our time. It is a standing rebuke to those who still confuse external ceremonialism with true religion. And it also gives the lie to those who assert that redemption in Christ has rendered the letter of the law obsolete and has released men from its binding claims. For the strange thing is that while the Pharisees turned the law into legal ceremonialism because they did not comprehend its relation to the grace of God, many Christians turn the grace of God into licence because they fail to appreciate its relation to the law.

How the idea should have arisen that grace has rendered the law unnecessary is difficult indeed to understand, for Paul states plainly that grace has been made available to man for the express purpose of enabling him to reach the divine standard, otherwise unattainable. "Do we then make void the law through faith?" he asks those who, in his day, put forth this strange notion, and quickly he answers, "God forbid; yea, we establish the law."

Elaborating this important truth later in this same epistle, the apostle says, "For what the law could not do, in that it was weak through the flesh, God sending His own Son in the likeness of sinful flesh, and for sin, condemned sin in the flesh: that the righteousness of the law might be fulfilled in us, who walk not after the flesh, but after the Spirit."

The law is God's eternal standard of righteousness. Not a jot nor a tittle was taken from it by Jesus during His life on earth, nor by His death on the cross. Jesus died in order to uphold its standards and His grace is imputed to man to blot out his transgression, and imparted to him in order that he may meet its demands.

It is quite wrong, therefore, to set the Old Testament in opposition to the New by calling one a dispensation of law and the other a dispensation of grace. Law and grace are not mutually exclusive. The one is God's eternal standard and the other is the only power by which man can rise to it.

In the great day of judgment, God's law will be the standard by which He will judge the lives of men. Those who will be privileged to eat of the tree of life will be those who, by grace and through faith, have kept all "His commandments."

This chapter is based on Matthew 5:17-37.

The Righteousness That Exceeds

THUS far in His Sermon on the Mount, Jesus had set forth the profound spiritual significance of the law and the real nature of sin. He had shown that, contrary to the teaching of the Pharisees, transgression of the law is not merely acted sin. Sin in the heart, like anger and lust, are no less iniquitous than the outward acts of murder and adultery.

Now Jesus goes on to explain that righteousness, like sin, is not an external standard of piety, but a condition of the heart. And in a series of vivid illustrations He contrasts the false righteousness of the Pharisees with the true righteousness which springs from faith in God, and which only can qualify men for a place in His kingdom.

The Pharisees, Jesus pointed out, made a great show of works of righteousness. To the sound of a trumpet, as it were, they bestowed their alms in the synagogues and in the streets that their benevolence might be publicized and gain the praise of men.

Men might be deceived by this ostentatious charity, said Jesus, but God is not. "Verily I say unto you, They have their reward." And when He said that He used the very expression which the tax collectors of that day put on their receipts. In the fleeting commendation of men, the Pharisees received "settlement in full" for their calculated benevolence. From the Father in heaven, therefore, they would receive no more.

How different is the true goodness which springs from love in the heart. It is not done for display, "to be seen of men." It matters not if it is unobserved .by men. Its reward is in the joy of the recipient and the approval of God, who sees "in secret" and will reward openly in His good time.

Again, said Jesus, the Pharisees "love to pray standing in the synagogues and in the corners of the streets." When the special times fixed for devotions came round

---

The Pharisees opposed Jesus because He taught that true goodness consists not in outward show, but springs from love in the heart.

By C. A. SLADE

they invariably arranged to be in some conspicuous place, where their loud-voiced piety might be observed by all. But this ostentatious devotion was not true prayer and their "vain repetitions" were of no more value than the incantations and magical formulæ recited by the heathen. The prayers of the Pharisees were heard only by men, and from men they had their "reward" in full.

The soul that truly longs for communion with God, on the other hand, will close his door upon the world, shut himself away from the eyes of men, and seek holy converse alone with Him. True, there is a place for public prayer as a corporate expression of devotion to God. But corporate prayer is no substitute for heart communion in solitude with God. Jesus often rose before it was day and stole away to some quiet retreat where He could pour out His soul in prayer to His Father in heaven. And if we would have power in our lives we must follow His example. For it is in secret prayer that the flood-tides of the power of God flow into the life.

Besides almsgiving and prayers, fasting also provided the Pharisees with frequent opportunities of giving visible evidence of their "righteousness." In the law of Moses there was actually only one occasion in the sanctuary year on which the people were commanded to fast, and that was on the day of atonement. The Pharisees, however, had multiplied fast days until there were no fewer than two every week. On Mondays and Thursdays they put on a "sad countenance," they "disfigured their faces" by leaving them unwashed and their beards untrimmed, and put ashes upon their heads. These outward acts brought them recognition as men of eminent piety, but it brought them no reward from God.

The one who truly seeks God by fasting and prayer, declared Jesus, will make no public show of his purpose. He will not even "appear unto men to fast." But God will see and from God he will receive the blessing he seeks.

Having revealed how far true devotion to God "exceeded" the hollow pretensions of the scribes and Pharisees, Jesus went on to show how far "exceeding" was the righteousness of the child of God in his relations with his fellow-men.

"Ye have heard that it hath been said, An eye for an eye, and a tooth for a tooth," Jesus reminded His hearers. In the days when this pronouncement was given to Israel fearful penalties were often inflicted by absolute rulers in the nations around for the most trivial of offences, and blood feuds were usually repaid with interest. To Israel, however, God decreed that no greater punishment was to be exacted for a crime against another than the offence merited.

In Christ's day the Pharisees congratulated themselves on their strict adherence to the letter of the law, but they revealed the lovelessness of their lives by demanding justice to the utmost farthing. If there had been in their hearts love for the transgressor they would have been ready to remit the proper demands of justice and even bear injustice if by this means reconciliation might be effected.

Suppose, for example, said Jesus, that an enemy "smite thee on thy right cheek." The demands of justice would require retaliation in the same measure. But a true child of God would offer the other cheek to shame the striker for his violence.

Under Jewish law a debtor might be required to forfeit his undergarment or coat in payment of a debt, but his cloak, or outer garment, could not be taken; or if it were, it would have to be returned by nightfall in order to preserve the wearer from the cold.

A Pharisee debtor would see that nothing more than the law permitted was taken from him. The true child of the Father, on the other hand, would offer his cloak voluntarily in a sincere effort to discharge his debt, and thereby the heart of the creditor might be softened and good relations restored.

One of the practices of the Romans in lands which they subjugated was to compel the able-bodied males, as well as their beasts, to act as baggage-bearers in the transport of supplies from station to station. It was in harmony with this custom that Simon was requisitioned to carry Christ's cross. The Romans generally limited such forced service to a Roman mile, but even this was resented by the proud Jews, and the grudging way in which they complied only made the Romans more determined to compel submission. But if the subject Jews had cheerfully offered to carry their loads an extra mile, relations between the Jews and Romans would doubtless have been ameliorated, and love would have proved itself more powerful than hate.

This is actually how God acts, in His love, toward sinful men. "He maketh His sun to rise on the evil and on the good," without discrimination, "and sendeth rain on the just and the unjust." Jesus loved the world even though it "received Him not," and for those who at last nailed Him to the cross, He prayed, "Father, forgive them; for they know not what they do." If, therefore, the love of God is in the hearts of His children they will love and pray for their enemies, too. "If ye love" only "them which love you, . . ." Jesus said, "do not even the publicans the same? And if ye salute your brethren only, what do ye more than others?" "I say unto you, Love your enemies, bless them that curse you, do good to them that hate you, and pray for them that despitefully use you and persecute you; that ye may be the children of your Father which is in heaven."

Thus Jesus contrasted the sham righteousness of the scribes and Pharisees with the "exceeding" righteousness which is a reflection of the character of God in the lives of His children.

The religion of the Pharisees, He showed, was not only valueless but an insult to God. Man might be deceived by it, but God, who looks not on the outward appearance but on the heart, called it by its right name, "hypocrisy." The term "hypocrite" was used in Christ's day for the masked actors in the Greek plays who simulated the characters they were intended to portray. By calling the Pharisees by this name, Jesus declared that, for all their profession, they were merely acting a part to create an impression. Theirs was a religion of pretence.

True religion, He emphasized, is not a round of outward observances, but the product of a heart relationship to God. What God looks for in the lives of His children is not a form of godliness, but a reproduction of His own character, "Be ye therefore perfect," said Jesus, "even as your Father which is in heaven is perfect."

This chapter is based on Matthew 5:38-6:8, 16-18.

CHAPTER FORTY

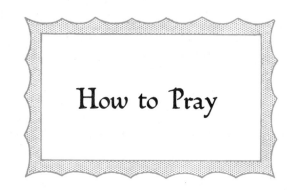

How to Pray

I T was the custom of religious teachers in the days of Jesus to instruct their disciples on how to approach God. As might be expected, the prayers of the scribes and Pharisees were as ostentatious and artificial as every other aspect of their religious life. Jesus referred in His Sermon on the Mount to their "much speaking" and their "vain repetitions." And, judging by the prayer of one Pharisee which is recorded in the gospels, they took delight in recounting to God all their virtues, and on the strength of their supposed righteousness they felt that they could claim a prompt answer to their petitions.

Jesus repudiated the idea that prayers are efficacious in proportion to their length or the fineness of their language. He taught that prayer is the language of the heart, not merely of the lips, and that God takes note of the sincerity of the prayer rather than the correctness of its outward form and expression.

The purpose of prayer is not to inform God about ourselves or even to acquaint Him with our needs, for He reads the secrets of our hearts and knows us better than we know ourselves. It is not so much to open the door of heaven's storehouse as to open the door of our hearts to permit a waiting God to come in and bless us.

The prayerless life is a deprived life because the door is kept fast shut against God. True prayer flings wide the doors of the heart to God and all the promises of His love.

Prayer is not so much to request God's services, as to beg Him to come in and order our lives according to His will.

These principles of true prayer Jesus taught in the wonderful model prayer which He gave to His disciples and which has ever since been called, "The Lord's Prayer." "Our Father, which art in heaven, hallowed be Thy name. Thy kingdom come.

Jesus taught His disciples how to approach God in a wonderful model prayer which has ever since been called, "The Lord's Prayer."   By C. NIELSON

21

Thy will be done in earth, as it is in heaven. Give us this day our daily bread. And forgive us our debts, as we forgive our debtors. And lead us not into temptation, but deliver us from evil: for Thine is the kingdom, and the power, and the glory, for ever. Amen."

"After this manner therefore pray ye," Jesus said, and in this remarkable prayer He reveals the attitude in which we should approach God and the kind of petitions which God delights to hear and answer. It is short and yet it comprehends all our needs, temporal and spiritual; it is simple yet it sounds the depths of God's redemptive grace.

Of course, any form of prayer, even the "Lord's prayer" can become a mere recitation, and so when we say it we should think of every phrase and pray it from our heart as well as with our lips.

"Our Father which art in heaven." The Pharisees portrayed God as a stern Law-giver and Judge, whose favour could be gained only by meticulous obedience to His commands. Jesus taught that God is the all-wise Creator and the omnipotent Ruler of the universe, but He also taught that He is the divine Father who loves to have His children around Him and delights to satisfy their every need.

You will notice that Jesus did not tell His disciples to pray, "My Father," but "Our Father." This was to impress upon their minds that all who acknowledge God as their Father are bound together in one family whatever their race or colour or language, whether they are rich or poor, wise or unlearned. The Pharisees were not prepared to think of the publicans as brethren, but Jesus called a publican to become one of His disciples. The Pharisees had "no dealings with the Samaritans," and they hated the Romans, but Jesus told His disciples that they were to be "witnesses" for Him in "Samaria, and unto the uttermost part of the earth."

What a difference it would make today if all men recognized God as their Father and themselves as brethren. It would eliminate all rivalry and strife and war. It would bring peace on earth and good will among men.

One of the ten commandments of the Decalogue is, "Honour thy father and thy mother." If we honour our earthly parents, how much more should we reverence our heavenly Father, who is the Creator and Ruler of all, and "hallow" His name. We honour our parents by upholding the family name, by recognizing their authority, and being obedient to their word. We hallow the name of our heavenly Father by giving reverence to Him in worship, by maintaining the honour of the heavenly family in our deportment, and by obedience to His commands. It was prophetically declared of Jesus, that He would say, "I delight to do Thy will, . . . yea, Thy law is within My heart," and so it will be also with all God's earthly children.

As the child of God senses the privilege and blessing of being a part of God's great family in heaven and earth, his heart will yearn for the return of all the prodigals who have been alienated by sin, and so he will constantly pray, "Thy kingdom come. Thy will be done in earth, as it is in heaven." This prayer is not just an expression of confidence that one day the "kingdoms of this world" will become "the kingdoms of our Lord, and of His Christ." If we really mean it, it is a prayer of surrender and self-dedication. It is first an invitation to God to come into our lives and begin His reign in us. It means, too, that we are ready to be used of God where and when and how He wills for the extension of His kingdom of grace in the hearts of men.

Having led the minds of the disciples, in the opening phrases of His model prayer, to a contemplation of the character of God and the vast scope of His purposes, Jesus next bade them pray, "Give us this day our daily bread." For He wanted them to realize that though God's rule is universal, infinite, and eternal, yet He is not forgetful of the daily needs of the least of His children.

This petition is an acknowledgment that He is the Source of all our benefits and that as we extend our hands in faith to receive, He stands waiting to give. So many accept God's bountiful provision for their physical needs without any sense of thankfulness or even recognition of the Source of their life. To sincerely pray, "Give us this day our daily bread," is gratefully to recognize with the Psalmist that God opens His hand and satisfies "the desire of every living thing."

Nor is this prayer only for temporal bread. Moses declared, "Man doth not live by bread only, but by every word that proceedeth out of the mouth of the Lord." In this prayer, therefore, we invite Him to provide also the spiritual Bread of life for our soul's need.

In the wilderness God gave manna to the Israelites a day at a time that they might never become forgetful of the Source of all their benefits. Jesus likewise bids us make our requests "daily" that we, too, may ever remember that all good gifts, temporal and spiritual, come from Him.

From man's daily sustenance, Jesus passes to his constant need of redemptive grace. "Forgive us our trespasses," He instructs us to pray. Though we may have sincerely given ourselves to Christ, all too often we take our eyes from Him, we let go His hand, and fall into sin. God is saddened by our falls from grace, but in His mercy He has made provision that if we "sin, we have an Advocate . . . Jesus Christ the righteous," and if we confess and truly repent of our waywardness, "He is faithful and just to forgive us our sins, and to cleanse us from all unrighteousness."

God makes only one condition for the bestowal of His forgiving grace and that is that we forgive those who transgress against us. "Forgive us our trespasses," we are to say, "as we forgive them that trespass against us." We can expect God to forgive us our trespasses only if we manifest a forgiving spirit toward those who injure us. As Jesus said in one of the Beatitudes, "Blessed are the merciful: for they shall obtain mercy."

To the request for forgiveness of sin, Jesus added a petition which has puzzled many: "And lead us not into temptation, but deliver us from evil." Surely it is Satan and not God who leads into temptation. If, however, we realize that the word "temptation" really means "testing," its meaning becomes clear. God does not lead into temptation, but He may see fit to lead us into the discipline of testing and trial.

OPPOSITE

A fishing boat on the beautiful, blue Sea of Galilee.

ABOVE

The village of Kefr Kenna, believed to be Cana of Galilee.

RIGHT

The modern city of Tiberias on the shores of the Sea of Galilee.

Jesus indicates in His prayer that it is perfectly proper to ask God to spare us the cup of testing and trial, for such a request is a confession of self-distrust and a desire not to fail under the test. Even Jesus prayed in Gethsemane that the cup of supreme suffering might, if possible, pass from Him. But to that prayer He added, "Nevertheless, not as I will, but as Thou wilt." If there was no other way, He was willing to submit to the will of His Father. And while we in like manner may pray, "If it be possible spare me from testing and trial," we should add, "But if it is for my good that I should be tried, then do Thou sustain me, for I know that by myself I shall fail." If we thus confess our own weakness and plead for His empowering grace, we may be sure that He will provide strength to bear every needful trial.

There may be a further meaning to this significant petition. While it is true that God does not lead any into temptation, if we resist His pleadings He may have to abandon us to Satan for a time to teach us that the way of the transgressor is hard. The apostle Paul speaks of one incorrigible sinner in Corinth, who had to be delivered "unto Satan for the destruction of the flesh, that the spirit may be saved in the day of the Lord Jesus." When, therefore, we make this petition we are pleading that, in spite of our wayward-ness, God may not abandon us, but bear with us until we are per-fectly surrendered to His will.

In the final phrase of His prayer, Jesus sets forth three reasons why we may look confidently to God to answer all our petitions: "For Thine is the kingdom, and the power, and the glory, for ever." God is seeking subjects for His kingdom of glory and He longs to make us worthy of a part in it. With Him is all power to deliver men from the kingdom of darkness and bring them into the kingdom of His dear Son. The crowning glory of God is redemption, and it is His purpose that, through the ages of eternity, we shall "show forth the praises of Him who hath called" us "out of darkness into His marvellous light."

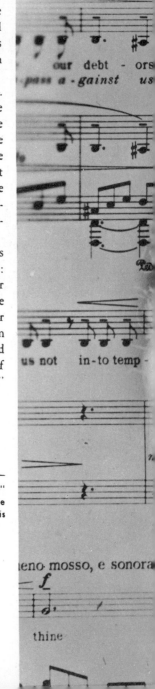

When we say the "Lord's Prayer" we should think of every phrase and pray it from the heart, as well as with our lips.

When we end our prayer "Amen" or "So be it," we are dedicating ourselves wholly to God and asking Him, from our hearts, to be to us all we need in this present life and to give us at last a part and a place in His completed purpose.

This chapter is based on Matthew 6:9-15; Luke 11:2-4.

The Two Ways

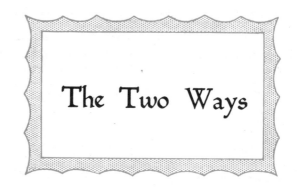

WHEN Moses declared God's purpose to Israel He said, "I call heaven and earth to record this day . . . that I have set before you life and death, blessing and cursing: therefore choose life, that both thou and thy seed might live."

In His wonderful sermon on the mountain in Galilee, Jesus set before His hearers, in a series of striking illustrations, the vital choice which the Gospel brings to men.

"No man can serve two masters," He said: "for either he will hate the one, and love the other; or else he will hold to the one, and despise the other. Ye cannot serve God and mammon."

When our first parents in Eden withdrew their loyalty from God by transgressing His commandment they became servants of Satan, foolishly believing that the wages he offered were better than the reward of loyalty to their Maker. And ever since man has had the choice of continuing in the service of Satan or giving his allegiance back to God.

In return for serving him Satan offers the "mammon of unrighteousness," and the "pleasures of sin." He can only offer them "for a season," however, because his tenure of office as "prince of this world" is strictly limited. When his lease expires he will lose everything and those who share his holdings will lose all too, including life itself.

God, on His part, makes no promise of possessions in "this present evil world." Instead He offers "the exceeding riches of His grace" and the "joy of His salvation," and promises to reserve for us in heaven an inheritance which "fadeth not away."

What a tragedy it is that so many are so short-sighted as to choose the baubles and tinsel of a world that "passeth away" in preference to becoming "heirs" with Christ in an eternal inheritance.

To all who come to Him in contrition of heart, Jesus offers the present joys of His salvation and the hope of eternal life.

By B. PLOCKHORST

There are those, of course, who imagine that they can make the best of both worlds. But they are sadly mistaken. It is not possible to divide the affections between God and mammon. If the thoughts are centred upon earthly things, God must inevitably be forgotten. If we would truly serve God, we must "love not the world, neither the things that are in the world." "Friendship of the world," Jesus declares, "is enmity with God." There is no neutrality and our choice is mutually exclusive.

In His second portrayal of the two choices offered to men, Jesus urged, "Lay not up for yourselves treasures upon earth . . . but lay up for yourselves treasures in heaven."

In saying this, Jesus did not mean that we should give no attention whatever to our material needs and the needs of those dependent upon us. God has arranged the seasons in order that we may sow and reap bountifully. He gives us "power to get wealth" and He expects us to be diligent in the use of our capacities. What He condemns is a false sense of values, a concentration of the thoughts and energies upon "laying up" treasure upon earth at the cost of neglecting fellowship with God. One man can become a millionaire and yet, if he regards his wealth as a sacred stewardship to be used to God's glory, he may maintain perfect fellowship with Him. Another might be cast down in spiritual ruin by a fraction of this wealth. It is when the "love of money" displaces love to God, and trust in material possessions is substituted for trust in God, that riches become the "root" from which all other "evil" springs.

Developing this illustration, Jesus went on to show how precarious, even in this life, is the "mammon of unrighteousness" which Satan offers to those who serve him.

"Lay not up for yourselves treasures upon earth," He said, "where moth and rust doth corrupt, and where thieves break through and steal." Just as the moth eats into the stored garment and rust corrodes strong metal till it crumbles to dust, so the foundations of earthly prosperity may be insidiously undermined and suddenly collapse. No "gilt edge" can guarantee the permanence of any earthly security.

It was a common practice in Jesus' day for thieves to tunnel through the mud-brick walls of the houses of the rich in search of treasure; even the great pyramids and the carefully hidden tombs of the Pharaohs were not proof against the wiles of the tomb robbers. There is, said Jesus, no real security in earthly possessions. And even though we may succeed in holding on to them in this life, the great thief, Death, triumphs in the end and robs us of all. How much wiser is it, therefore, to store up the treasures of pardon and peace in heaven's safe-keeping by loyalty to God and obedience to His commandments, that they may stand to our account when we pass from this world into the world to come.

But, some may say, if we forsake the world and all it offers and give to God our undivided allegiance, if our thoughts are centred upon the advancement of His cause and the coming of His kingdom, how shall we fare in respect of our temporal needs? For answer, Jesus pointed to the birds which circled and wheeled above the heads of the multitude as they listened.

"Behold the fowls of the air," He said: "for they sow not, neither do they reap, nor gather into barns; yet your heavenly Father feedeth them." The fact that God brought these creatures into existence to fill the air with their carols of praise, proclaims His intention to sustain their lives for the fulfilment of that purpose. If God has a far higher purpose for our lives, surely He will have no less care for us as we seek to realize our high calling in Christ.

Again, said Jesus, motioning with His hand to the green hillside bright with flowers of many hues, "Consider the lilies of the field, how they grow; they toil not, neither do they spin: and yet I say unto you, That even Solomon in all his glory was not arrayed like one of these." God decks the flowers of hill and dale, of meadow and river bank, in all their loveliness to add beauty to the face of the earth. But if He goes to such pains to make a thing of beauty like a flower, "which today is, and tomorrow" is fuel for the cooking "oven," can He not be trusted to provide for the needs of those for whom He has planned a far higher and more enduring destiny?

In the very bodies that God has given to us we have evidence of His care. "Which of you," Jesus asked, "by taking thought can add one cubit unto his stature?" Physical growth takes place because God has planned that we reach a certain development. Far more important than this is the spiritual stature He would have us attain. Will He then be less ready to supply all that will contribute to that end?

Drawing yet again from the familiar scenes of daily life Jesus went on: "What man is there of you, whom if his son ask bread, will he give him a stone? Or if he ask a fish, will he give him a serpent? If ye then, being evil, know how to give good gifts to your children, how much more shall your Father which is in heaven give good things to them that ask Him?" here in this present life, and even more abundantly in the life to come.

"Ask," He added in a wonderful three-fold promise, "and it shall be given you," for His ear is quick to catch the faintest cry of His children and His hand is open to satisfy their every need. "Seek, and ye shall find," for He is near to bless. "Knock, and it shall be opened unto you," for His hand is upon the door waiting to answer your call.

If we need not be anxious about today's needs, even less need we worry about tomorrow's. He who "knows the end from the beginning" can be trusted to care for tomorrow when tomorrow comes. So, said Jesus, "Take no [anxious] thought for your life, what ye shall eat, or what ye shall drink; nor yet for your body, what ye shall put on. . . . Seek ye first the kingdom of God, and His righteousness," and all your lesser needs will not be forgotten.

The thoughts of the worldly are bounded by their temporal needs because this life is all that is certain to them. But in God's purpose, this life is only an anteroom to a far greater and more enduring existence. And if your thoughts and energies are directed to that high destiny, God will see that you lack nothing which will contribute to your attaining to it.

In one last vivid illustration Jesus contrasted the end of those who travel the "broad" road of worldly pleasure and sinful ease, with those who take the "narrow" and upward way which leads to God.

Palestine is a land of hills and valleys, and doubtless from where He stood Jesus could glimpse the broad highway leading across the Gennesaret plain and the thin white threads of hill paths climbing steeply to villages perched upon the mountain tops.

As He looked He saw the broad road thronged with people, while crowding the inns along the way the more leisured travellers regaled themselves with wine and song. How appropriate a picture this was of the multitudes who choose the broad way in life, thinking only of the ease of the journey and the pleasures by the way. And how significant, too, were the solitary figures who turned from the broad road to climb the upward way to the hills.

As the eyes of the listening throng followed the crowds along the broad road and the little figures pressing on their upward way, Jesus drove home His warning: "Wide is the gate, and broad is the way that leadeth to destruction, and many there be that go in thereat;" while "straight is the gate, and narrow is the way which leadeth unto life, and few there be that find it." How sad it is that so many should choose what seems the broad and pleasant way of self-indulgence, little realizing that it ends in bondage, pain, sorrow, and death. How much better the choice of those who turn through the strait gate into the narrow road which leads to the city of God. True, it means surrendering all worldly ambition and forsaking its vanities and its sins. It is a rugged and a difficult road and constant care is needed to avoid the pitfalls beside the way. It takes diligence and perseverance to press always on and up. But along the upward road are living springs of God's providence and care. There are resting places where the soul finds refreshment and revival. There is a Guide who blazes the trail before us, and ever brighter grows the path as it nears the golden gate of the city of God.

Happy indeed are those who choose the upward way and reach the eternal city of refuge before earth's sunset when the gates are shut.

This chapter is based on Matthew 6:19-34; 7:7-14; Luke 11:9-13, 34-36; 12:22-30; 16:13.

CHAPTER
FORTY-TWO

The House on the Rock

THE chief characteristic of the Pharisees, as Jesus more than once pointed out, was spiritual pride. In the synagogues they coveted the chief places. On the streets and in the market places they paraded their piety, and in their prayers they did not hesitate to recount to God all their supposed virtues.

Second only to their spiritual pride, and indeed a consequence of it, was their critical spirit toward others. When they were not proclaiming their own righteousness they were passing judgment upon someone else. So Jesus appropriately devoted the closing remarks of His great discourse on the mount to the subject of judgment, human and divine.

Those who judge the motives of others, He declared, need to be very careful that they do not lay themselves open to being judged by the same standard and coming off worst! For be assured, He said, "that with what judgment ye judge, ye shall be judged: and with what measure ye mete, it shall be measured to you again."

"Why," Jesus went on, addressing particularly the Pharisees in His audience, "beholdest thou the mote," or little splinter .of wood, "that is in thy brother's eye, but considerest not" the veritable "beam, that is in thine own eye?" If they must judge others they would be well advised first to "cast out the beam" from their own eye; then they would be able to see clearly to "cast out the mote" from their brother's eye.

Better still is it, Jesus said, if we do not set ourselves up as judges of others. "Judge not, that ye be not judged." For while we may and should recognize sin for what it is, God alone can read the motives of the human heart. Moreover, as the Father "hath committed all judgment unto the Son," those who take it upon themselves to pass premature judgment on others, are usurping not only the place of God, but of Christ also.

But while it is neither our prerogative nor within our capacity to judge others, men do actually judge themselves by their acts. As surely as a tree reveals its nature

33

by its fruit, the real character will manifest itself in the fruit of the life. "By their fruits," said Jesus, "ye shall know them."

It is in the nature of a tree to bear fruit "after its kind." Thorns will not bear luscious grapes, nor will thorns, thistles, or brambles produce figs. If a tree is a good tree at its heart it will bear good fruit, while if a tree is poisonous by nature it will bear poisonous fruit. Just as trees cannot help showing by their fruit what they are, neither can men. For a time, like wheat and tares in the early stages of growth, the good and the evil may be almost indistinguishable, but sooner or later the time comes when the real character is revealed in the fruit of their doings. We judge the value of a tree by the fruit it yields and the final test of the lives of men is not their profession, but the fruit which they bear.

This is not a contradiction of the constant teaching of the Bible that men are saved not by works but by faith. It simply means that if a man is truly a child of God by faith he cannot help but do the things which please God. If his life is rooted in faith, the fruits of righteousness will be seen. Conversely, if the fruits of righteousness are not manifest in the life, there must be something wrong at the heart, for out of the heart are the "issues of life."

We do not need, therefore, to judge men. They invariably judge themselves, and as Jesus said, "By their fruits ye shall know them." Even so, Jesus went on to explain, there may be some who so cleverly conceal their real character as to completely deceive their fellow-men. They may even achieve distinction in the church of God, speaking in His name and doing exploits in His cause. But though in this life their deception may seem to be successful, it is supreme folly for them to imagine that in the final test they will deceive God.

Perhaps Jesus was thinking of Judas, who was standing with the other disciples, when He solemnly declared: "Not every one that saith unto Me, Lord, Lord, shall enter into the kingdom of heaven; but he that doeth the will of My Father which is in heaven."

Right up to the night of the last supper Judas deceived his fellow disciples. But he never deceived Jesus and when they gathered for that farewell meal Jesus exposed the evil heart which had long lain beneath the suave exterior.

It was a fearful shock to the other disciples to realize that the betrayer had been in their midst all the time. And doubtless it would be a great shock to the church of God today if the real character of some in their midst were revealed. For, declared Jesus, "Many will say to Me in that day, Lord, Lord, have we not prophesied in Thy name? and in Thy name cast out devils? and in Thy name done many wonderful works?" "And then," He added sadly, "will I profess unto them, I never knew you: depart from Me, ye that work iniquity."

Solemn indeed is the realization that in the day of judgment many who have been respected as members of His church and leaders in His cause will hear the dread pronouncement, "I never knew you," and all their works will be revealed as a mere profession covering a sinful heart. Unlike Judas these "betrayers" may never be exposed in this life, but in the day of God's judgment the secrets of all hearts will be laid bare. Doubtless there will also be many in that day, who have been spurned by these hypocritical make-believers, but who will be welcomed by Jesus into the joy of the Lord.

In a final dramatic illustration Jesus brought His sermon to a close by showing how the true and the false will finally be manifest. "Whosoever heareth these sayings of Mine, and doeth them," He said, "I will liken him unto a wise man which built his house upon a rock," while "every one that heareth these sayings of Mine, and doeth them not, shall be likened unto a foolish man, which built his house upon the sand."

Among the hills of Galilee there are many watercourses which, during the rainless season, are completely dried up, leaving wide stretches of the sandy river bottom exposed. Jesus pictured a foolish builder coming upon one of these level reaches beside a stream and thinking how easy it would be to build his house upon such a ready prepared site. And so, without worrying about foundations, he erected a splendid edifice which earned the admiration of all who saw it.

The other man was wise enough to realize that a structure is only as enduring as its foundations and so, turning his back upon the tempting level beach, he sought, on higher ground, a rock foundation for his home.

He was chided by the foolish builder for going up so high when there was plenty of room along the river bank, and for expending his energies in levelling the hard rock when there were sites by the river needing no preparation at all. But the wise man went on preparing his foundation and then digging deep into the rock to anchor the walls. Hard he toiled, carrying all the materials up to the top of the rock, but at last his building was also finished.

There seemed not much to choose between the two buildings so far as their outward appearance was concerned while the summer lasted. But soon the rainy season came and the wintry winds began to blow In a very little time the dry river bed had become a raging torrent. With alarm the foolish builder saw the flood swirling round the base of his house, churning up what had so recently been a firm beach. Before long the house on the sand was undermined and collapsed with a great crash. All the while, the house of the wise man high up on the rocky bank was safe from the swirling waters. Secure against wind and rain it stood upon its firm base, and when the house of the foolish man had been broken up and swept away the wise man's house remained.

So, concluded Jesus, will it be when the lives of men are put to the final test. Those who have been satisfied with a mere form or appearance of godliness, will fail to stand up to the stern trials of life and the still sterner judgments of God when He shakes terribly the earth. In that day all that can be shaken will be shaken and removed, and only "those things which cannot be shaken" will remain.

The only life that will endure for time and eternity is one which is built upon the sure foundation of Christ and around a heart wholly surrendered and obedient to Him.

This chapter is based on Matthew 7 :1-5, 15-27: Luke 6 :37-49.

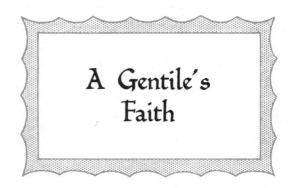

CHAPTER
FORTY-THREE

A Gentile's Faith

WHEN Jesus ended His teachings on the mountain-side near Capernaum, He returned with His disciples to the city. The news that Jesus was back again spread quickly through the town. It reached, among others, the ears of a certain centurion who was stationed there. He may have been an officer of the Roman garrison based on Capernaum, or perhaps, more likely, in the service of Herod Antipas, the tetrarch of Galilee, whose security forces were organized on Roman lines and officered by Greeks or Romans.

Though he had been brought up a pagan, this centurion, since his appointment to Palestine, had been attracted to the Jewish faith, like Cornelius the Roman centurion of Joppa, and had become a "proselyte of the gate." That is, although he was not circumcised and did not conform to all the rabbinical regulations, he believed in the true God, observed the precepts of the moral law, and worshipped in the Jewish synagogue.

Being a man of considerable means, he had actually built a synagogue for the Jews in Capernaum, perhaps the very one whose ruins are still scattered along the shore of the lake at Tell Hum. In this building, indeed, there are decorative features in Græco-Roman style which may have been incorporated as a mark of appreciation to the donor.

Apparently the centurion had never met Jesus, but he had heard of His wonderful works. When he learned that Jesus was near, he was impressed to seek His help on behalf of a greatly esteemed servant who was grievously ill with a painful paralytic affection that had brought him to the point of death. The distress of the centurion for his servant shows him to have been a good man, for in those days slaves were regarded merely as chattels to be cast aside without any feeling when they ceased to be

---

Hearing of His wonderful works, a Roman centurion comes to ask Jesus to heal a faithful servant.

of use. Perhaps this servant had saved his master's life in battle. Or, if he were a Jew, he might even have been instrumental in bringing to the centurion a knowledge of God. Whatever the reason, he was greatly attached to his servant and, when all human help failed, his thoughts turned to the great Healer, Jesus.

Doubtless, the centurion had heard of the healing of the nobleman's son at Cana some time before, but so humble-spirited was this kindly and devout man that he did not feel worthy to approach Jesus personally. Instead he sought out the elders of the local synagogue and asked them to intercede for him. The elders were only too ready to help so influential a patron and at once set off to find Jesus.

Their pharisaic approach was evident in the presentation of the centurion's request, for they started out by telling how "worthy" a man he was and how deserving of Jesus' help. "He loveth our nation," they urged, "and hath built us a synagogue."

But Jesus was not like the Pharisees. He did not ask what good deeds those who came to Him had done. It was sufficient for Him if they came believing that He cared for them and would grant their requests. On this occasion, therefore, He was influenced, not by the recital of the centurion's good deeds, admirable as they had been, but by his faith and the humility of his approach.

Readily Jesus set off with the elders for the centurion's house. When the news of His approach reached the officer, his first thought was that his house was not ceremonially clean enough for a great. Rabbi to enter. So he sent friends to meet Jesus, saying, "Lord, trouble not Thyself: for I am not worthy that Thou shouldest enter under my roof." To Jesus the centurion's sense of unworthiness was the best evidence he could give of his worthiness, and so He continued on His way.

Still anxious that Jesus should not find anything in his house to offend Him, the centurion himself hurried out as He approached. Renewing his apologies for bringing Jesus out of His way, he said, "Say in a word, and my servant shall be healed."

"For," he went on, "I also am a man set under authority, having under me soldiers, and I say unto one, Go, and he goeth; and to another, Come, and he cometh; and to my servant, Do this, and he doeth it." If he, a Roman officer, had only to command those under him to secure immediate obedience, surely Jesus who exercised the power of God, needed only to say the word and his servant's disease would depart.

When Jesus compared the faith of this Gentile soldier with the unbelief and opposition He had met among His own countrymen, "He marvelled," and, turning to the people who followed Him, He said, "I have not found so great faith, no, not in Israel. And I say unto you, That many shall come from the east and west, and shall sit down with Abraham, and Isaac, and Jacob, in the kingdom of heaven. But the children of the kingdom shall be cast out into outer darkness: there shall be weeping and gnashing of teeth."

The Jews had a tradition that in the day of Messiah's triumph He would "spread a great table" for the Jews, while the Gentiles would look on and "be ashamed." What a shock it must have been for the proud Pharisees when Jesus reversed the picture and declared that the believing Gentiles would be sitting in the places they thought were reserved for them, while they would be cast out into "darkness." This was indeed "new teaching" and most unwelcome to them. But Jesus did not wait for their comments. He turned to the centurion and said, "Go thy way; and as thou hast believed, so be it done unto thee."

Joyfully the officer hurried back to his house to find that his servant had been restored "in the selfsame hour" that Jesus had spoken the healing word. We may be sure that not only physical healing but salvation also came to his house that day.

That this miracle should immediately follow Jesus' teaching about the kingdom and its subjects in His Sermon on the Mount is surely most significant, for, in the experience of this first Gentile who came to Christ, we have an assurance of the universality of salvation. Though not belonging to Israel after the flesh, the centurion was truly of the company of spiritual Israel who were to come "from the east and west" and from the north and south through the witness of the Gospel.

In that little group, with the centurion and his companions standing with the disciples before Jesus, we have a picture in miniature of God's children of all nations who will one day be united in the kingdom of heaven.

This chapter is based on Luke 7:1-10; Matthew 8:5-13.

The centurion was the first Gentile to come to Christ.

By Wm. HOLE

Back from the Dead

SOON after healing the centurion's, servant, Jesus set out on a second missionary tour of the cities of Galilee, which was to occupy much of the autumn of A.D. 29.

On His first itinerary only His earliest disciples were with Him. Now He had the companionship and help of all the twelve He had ordained. For these, it was a priceless lesson in missionary service which they were soon to put to practical use.

With Jesus also were "certain women" who had become disciples, and gladly ministered in various ways to the needs of Jesus and the disciples on their travels. Among those mentioned by name were Mary of Magdala, out of whom Jesus had cast seven devils, Joanna, the wife of Herod's steward Chuza, and Susanna. The two latter were evidently women of means who kept the common purse of the disciple band supplied out of "their substance" in return for the spiritual benefits they had received from Jesus.

Just what route Jesus took as He "went throughout every city and village, preaching and showing the glad tidings of the kingdom of God" we do not know, but it may have been during the early part of this journey that He met the two blind men who cried after Him, "Thou Son of David, have mercy on us."

Not wishing to enter into another controversy with His ever-watching enemies over His Messiahship, which the physically blind men had clearly discerned with their spiritual eyes, Jesus drew them aside into a house, doubtless one in which He had found temporary hospitality.

"Believe ye that I am able to do this?" He asked the men when He had them to Himself. "Yea, Lord," they replied with one voice. Thereupon, in response to their faith Jesus touched their eyes and "their eyes were opened."

As they left rejoicing, Jesus bade them say nothing of what He had done so that

In raising the widow's son to life again at Nain, Jesus gave a crowning demonstration of His divine power.
By ANKER LUND

He might be free to go on to other cities, but they could not keep their blessing to themselves and crowds followed Him on His journey as His fame was spread abroad.

After a circuitous journey of some weeks through the countryside of Galilee, Jesus and His disciples came down from the highlands by the rocky road skirting Mount Tabor and reached the eastern end of the plain of Esdraelon. It was approaching evening when the little party began to climb the steep hill path leading to the village of Nain.

The name of the village, which means "fair," indicates its delightful situation upon a tableland on the north-western slopes of Little Hermon which towered upward to a height of some 1,500 feet. Westward, the plain of Esdraelon, green and beautiful with springing crops, stretched away to the sea, bounded by the blue Carmel range to the south and the hills of Lower Galilee on the other side. Today the situation of the village is as "fair" as it ever was, for the fertile plain is now dotted with Jewish settlements of the new state of Israel, but the modern village of Nain itself is a squalid hamlet surrounded by the poor fields of the Moslem inhabitants.

The shadows were lengthening as Jesus and His disciples passed a number of rock caves which served as the cemetery of Nain. Some had already received their complement of dead and were sealed to prevent the entrance of wild animals. The black depths of others gaped wide as if waiting to close in upon their victims.

They had just left the rock sepulchres behind when a sound of wailing came from the gate of the town, and a funeral procession emerged. There was nothing unusual about this, however, for it was customary for the burial of the dead to take place just before nightfall.

At the head of the procession was the one appointed to pronounce the funeral oration at the tomb. Behind him were the hired woman mourners, wailing their dirge of lament. Then came four bearers carrying a simple bier of wood and wickerwork upon which lay the inanimate form of a young man wrapped in a linen shroud. A napkin was lightly laid over the upturned face and the pale, bloodless hands were folded upon the breast. Behind the bier, supported by friends from the village, was his mother, an elderly widow, overcome with grief at the loss of her only son.

Their destination was one of the rock caves down the road where the widow, some time before, had laid her husband, the father of the dead boy. There the body would be placed in a rock niche, the funeral oration would be delivered, the entrance of the cave would be blocked up again, and the poor mother, the last of the family, would return to her empty home and her sorrow. But on this calm autumn evening events were not to take their accustomed course.

Thinking that Jesus and His disciples were strangers seeking lodging in the city for the night, the bereaved mother hardly looked at them as she passed. But as Jesus read the tragedy in the frail, bent form, He said gently to her, "Weep not."

For an instant she lifted her eyes in gratitude for the word of sympathy and was about to walk on when Jesus stepped forward and touched the bier, motioning the bearers to stop.

Recognizing Him as a rabbi they could not conceal their surprise that He should incur ceremonial defilement by this act, seeing that He had no connection with the family of the dead youth. A moment later their surprise was turned to amazement when Jesus addressed the lifeless form upon the bier. "Young man," He cried in a voice of authority, which resounded in the still evening air, "I say unto thee, Arise."

No sooner had He spoken than there was a movement of the hands of the young man, then he raised his head. and a moment later was sitting up.

Helping him down from the bier, Jesus led the youth to his astonished mother, who was as overcome with emotion at the embrace of her restored child as she had been a few minutes before, mourning for his death.

The first effect of the miracle upon the crowd was fear at the wondrous thing which they had seen. Then, when they had recovered from their amazement, they began to "glorify God" saying, "A great prophet is risen up among us; . . . God hath visited His people."

Without a doubt their thoughts went back to the miracle which Elisha wrought centuries before at Shunem, over on the other side of this very mountain, when he brought another widow's son back to life.

If these people had stopped to think they would have realized that Jesus was not just another "prophet," for the manner in which He raised the widow's son of Nain was quite different from the miracle of Elisha in Shunem or that of Elijah who raised the widow's son of Zarephath, in Phœnicia.

When Elisha came into the house of the Shunamite he "shut the door . . . and prayed unto the Lord." When Elijah took the dead son of the widow of Zarephath from her bosom and carried him to the room where he dwelt, he also "cried unto the Lord." But Jesus did not intercede with God for this widow's son, He authoritatively bade the boy, "Arise," and life instantaneously animated the dead body.

Here was no "prophet" claiming the power of God on behalf of a poor widow. Jesus was Himself God speaking life into the body of the widow's son as, in the beginning, He breathed into Adam the breath of life and made him a "living soul."

But the eyes of the people were holden and only by the intimate circle of the disciples was this miracle seen as the crowning evidence that Jesus was the Son of God. Already He had shown His power over the inanimate creation by turning water into wine. He had revealed His power over disease by healing multitudes of all manner of physical and mental afflictions. He had put Satan's minions to rout by casting devils out of those who were possessed. Now, for the first time, He revealed His ultimate power by opening the gates of death and bringing one of its victims back to life again.

But why did Jesus wait until now to give this crowning demonstration of His power? The answer surely lies in the events which had recently preceded it. On the mount Jesus had inaugurated His kingdom and chosen its first witnesses. In the healing of the centurion's servant He had shown that the subjects of the kingdom would come from the east and the west, from the north and the south, to sit with Abraham and Isaac and Jacob in glory. Now, in the raising of the widow's son of Nain, He revealed

His power to bring back even from the grave those who believed in Him, to have a part in His kingdom.

It is significant, too, that this was the first miracle which Jesus wrought unbidden. He had healed multitudes who came to Him asking for relief. He had helped many on the earnest intercession of friends. But on this occasion the initiative was His alone. Why? Because that is how, in the great day of His coming, He will call the dead from their dusty beds. At the command of His Father He will descend from the heavens and, with a shout of triumph, He will call forth the believing dead from their graves.

"The hour cometh," declared Jesus on another occasion, "in the which all that are in the graves shall hear His voice, and shall come forth."

"In a moment, in the twinkling of an eye, at the last trump," asserts the apostle Paul, "the dead shall be raised." "For the Lord Himself shall descend from heaven with a shout, with the voice of the Archangel, and with the trump of God: and the dead in Christ shall rise."

As Jesus restored this boy to his mother, many children separated by death will then be restored to their parents and parents to their children. With cries of joy parents will clasp their children to their bosoms. Children will again embrace their loved ones.

Death will be completely swallowed up in victory and every tear will be wiped away.

No wonder Paul ends his thrilling description of the resurrection of the last day with the exhortation: "Comfort one another with these words."

And well we may, for the miracle of the raising of the widow's son was the first of many evidences that Jesus was to give that not even the death of the body will keep His people from one another and from His kingdom in the day when the "meek shall inherit the earth."

This chapter is based on Matthew 9:27-31; Luke 7:11-17.

As Jesus restored this boy to his mother, so in the resurrection day loved ones, separated by death, will be joyfully reunited.

By J. M. H. HOFMANN

Releasing Sin's
Captives

FROM Nain, Jesus made His way with His disciples back toward the Sea of Galilee and it was probably as He neared the lake that there was brought to Him a blind and dumb demoniac, from whom, to the amazement of the crowd, Jesus expelled the evil spirit.

Among the people who stood by there were, as usual, malicious scribes and Pharisees who immediately suggested that it was by Beelzebub, "the prince of devils," that Jesus cast out evil spirits.

Beelzebub was originally the Philistine god of flies, but, by the time of Jesus, it had come to be credited with power over disease in general and was worshipped by the heathen of Galilee and Syria.

Usually, Jesus took no notice of the enemies who followed Him everywhere, but this blasphemous attack called for a prompt reply. Turning to His accusers, Jesus asked them if it was conceivable that Satan would permit his subordinates to possess their poor victims and then discredit them by using Him, Jesus, to cast them out? Surely, He said, "If a kingdom be divided against itself, that kingdom cannot stand. And if a house is divided against itself, that house cannot stand. And if Satan rise up against himself, and be divided, he cannot stand, but hath an end." Their explanation, therefore, was foolish in the extreme.

Following up His argument, Jesus asked them a further pointed question: "If I by Beelzebub cast out devils, by whom do your children cast them out?" There were in Christ's day many Jewish exorcists who professed by their incantations to cast out evil spirits. Obviously, then, the argument that the Pharisees used against Jesus would apply equally to them. If He was in league with Satan, they must be in league with him, too!

If, on the other hand, they claimed that the power of God was with them, Jesus, who cast out devils not by long incantations but by His simple command, surely exercised far more powerfully the "finger of God." Is it not evident then, said Jesus, that in Me "the kingdom of God is come unto you."

To press His point home Jesus used a vivid illustration. "When a strong man armed keepeth his palace, his goods are in peace, but when a stronger than he shall come upon him, and overcome him, he taketh from him all his armour wherein he trusted, and divideth his spoils."

Satan is the "strong man armed" and his "palace" is the world, for he is the "god of this world." "His goods" are the victims who have fallen into his clutches, and "his armour" includes all the evil devices whereby he holds men enslaved.

But Jesus is "stronger" than Satan and the great purpose of His coming was to "preach deliverance to the captives" and to "set at liberty" those in bondage to Satan. It was by virtue of His divine power that He had released this poor victim before Him.

On a later occasion Jesus completely turned the tables upon His Pharisee accusers by telling them that it was not He but they who were in league with Satan. "Ye are of your father the devil," He plainly declared.

Jesus' work of releasing the captives of Satan was the subject of one of the wonderful prophecies of Isaiah. In response to the inspired question, "Shall the prey be taken from the mighty?" Jesus prophetically answered, "Thus saith the Lord, Even the captives of the mighty shall be taken away, and the prey of the terrible shall be delivered: for I will contend with him that contendeth with thee, and I will save thy children. . . . And all flesh shall know that I the Lord am thy Saviour and thy Redeemer."

When He walked among men, Jesus frequently showed that He was stronger than Satan, and today He is still despoiling the devil of his prey. His work may not always be as spectacular as when He cast out the dumb spirit before the scribes and Pharisees, but there are countless souls who can testify to equally effective deliverance from spiritual bondage.

Having conclusively rebutted the Pharisees' accusation as to the source of His power, Jesus took the opportunity they had given Him of sounding a further warning about Satan's devices. The power of God, He said, is ever available to deliver men from Satan's cruel bondage, but unless those who are delivered invite Him to abide with them always, they leave themselves open to further and even more fearful attacks.

"When the unclean spirit is gone out of a man," He explained, "he walketh through dry places, seeking rest" in some other victim. "Finding none," he says to himself, "I will return unto my house whence I came out."

Coming to the soul whom he once held in bondage for his master, Satan, he finds his heart "swept and garnished," but empty because of the failure of the delivered one to receive the abiding presence of Jesus.

So, continued Jesus, he goeth "and taketh to him seven other spirits more wicked than himself; and they enter in, and dwell there: and the last state of that man is worse than the first."

The Pharisees themselves were an example of what Jesus meant, for while they had allowed the truth of God, through Moses and the prophets, to cleanse their lives from the idolatries of the heathen, their refusal to receive Jesus into their lives had exposed them to new satanic deceptions.

Only the abiding presence of Christ can garrison the heart and life against the assaults of Satan. Without His constant presence we are at the mercy of our spiritual foes. But with Him we are "more than conquerors."

As the shamefaced Pharisees slunk away before His withering condemnation, Jesus followed them with a final warning.

"Verily I say unto you," He declared, "All sins shall be forgiven unto the sons of men, and blasphemies wherewith soever they shall blaspheme: but he that shall blaspheme against the Holy Ghost hath never forgiveness, but is in danger of eternal damnation."

In earlier days God had used many means to reveal His love and draw rebellious Israel back to Him. He had revealed Himself in His works and through His prophets, but their witness was rejected. By sending His Son, God revealed His willingness to overlook and forgive their sin. But they were now rejecting Him. Still God was merciful and gracious, and forgiveness would be granted to them if they repented of their transgression. Even on the cross Jesus prayed for those who crucified Him saying: "Father, forgive them; for they know not what they do." But if they finally rejected the pleadings of the Holy Spirit who would be sent when He returned to His Father, there would be no further opportunity. That is why the writer of the epistle to the Hebrews pleads, "Today if ye will hear His voice, harden not your hearts."

In our day the Spirit is making His final appeal to the hearts of men. Sometimes people are troubled by the feeling that they have already committed the unpardonable sin and have been rejected by God. The very fact, however, that their conscience is stirred by a sense of guilt is evidence that the Spirit is still pleading and that salvation awaits the response of the heart and will.

But soon the Spirit will cease to strive and man's probation will come to an end. Then those who have rejected God's last message of mercy will indeed face eternal loss.

More urgent than ever before, therefore, is the appeal of the Spirit: "Today if ye will hear His voice, harden not your hearts." May none who read these words fail to respond.

This chapter is based on Matthew 12:22-45; Mark 3:20-30; Luke 11:14-32.

God's Great Family

SINCE Jesus was expelled by the angry mob from the synagogue at Nazareth, His mother and family had not seen Him. But from time to time news reached them from friends in Capernaum of His incessant labours.

His brethren still did not recognize Him as the promised Messiah and His condemnation of the religious leaders of the day had brought them great embarrassment. When finally they heard that the Pharisees had charged Him with being "possessed" of a devil the reproach was too much for them. They determined to go to Capernaum, and, if necessary, forcibly restrain Him.

Realizing that Jesus would not be likely to listen to them they confided their fears to Mary and asked her to go and help them. At first she hesitated, for though Joseph's children did not believe, she knew that Jesus was the divine Son and that in all He did He was guided and sustained by His heavenly Father. But as they became more and more insistent, she at last consented to accompany them.

When they arrived in Capernaum and inquired after Jesus they were directed to the house where He lodged. Hurrying there they found, as usual, the courtyard thronged with listeners and afflicted ones who had come seeking His healing touch. They tried to force their way through the milling crowd, but it was impossible. At last, through the disciples, they managed to get a message to Jesus that His mother and brethren were outside seeking Him. They particularly mentioned Mary, feeling that He would want to see her, even if they could expect little regard from Him.

In the brief account of the incident recorded for us it might seem that Jesus treated the message rather unceremoniously, but, of course, He did not. Though He knew that His brethren were thinking only of themselves He certainly must have called His mother to Him and assured her that she had nothing to fear for Him. All

God's great family takes in men and women, boys and girls, of every race, and language, and colour.

through His life Jesus had treated Mary with the most tender solicitude and almost His last act as He hung in agony upon the cross, was to commend her to the care of His beloved disciple, John.

But, as He so often used the happenings of the moment to impress some lesson upon His hearers, the message which was brought to Him on this occasion provided an opportunity to teach a profound spiritual truth.

"Who is My mother, and who are My brethren?" He asked the assembled company. According to the flesh Mary was His mother and those with whom He had grown up in the little home at Nazareth were His brethren. But because God was His real Father, He had a far wider family relationship with all who were truly children of God.

Looking round on them that "sat about Him," He said, "Behold My mother and My brethren! For whosoever shall do the will of My Father which is in heaven, the same is My brother, and sister, and mother."

By this declaration Jesus was not disowning His earthly family, whom He dearly loved, but He was saying that all who turned from their sins and surrendered their lives to Him were "born again" into the family of God. They might be Jews or Samaritans or Gentiles according to the flesh, but if they became His followers they were children of His heavenly Father and He was "not ashamed" to call them brethren and sisters.

They might be rich and influential, they might be publicans and sinners, yet they were all members of the family of God.

The apostle Paul explains this wonderful new family relationship when he writes: "For as many as are led by the Spirit of God, they are the sons of God. For ye have not received the spirit of bondage again to fear; but ye have received the spirit of adoption [sonship], whereby we cry, Abba, Father."

Ever since Christ's day this great family of God has been growing, until now it takes in men and women, boys and girls, of every race and language and colour. All are equally dear to the heart of God and should be to one another.

In many ways our earthly relationships help us to understand those which should obtain in God's great spiritual family. More than once Jesus compared the love of an earthly father with God's care for His children, assuring us, however, that God's love is infinitely greater than the love of even the best of earthly parents. "If ye then, being evil," He said, "know how to give good gifts unto your children, how much more shall your Father which is in heaven give good things to them that ask Him?"

If the love of our earthly parents constrains us to honour and obey them, how much more should we honour and obey our heavenly Father?

If there is love and devotion between the members of an earthly family, should we not love equally dearly those who are united with us in spiritual fellowship in the family of God? And how ready we should be to serve one another in the bonds of Christian love.

Because we are proud of the earthly family to which we belong we are careful always to maintain its honour. Should we not be even more anxious to uphold the honour of the family of God, avoiding any word or action which would besmirch its fair name?

It is, of course, God's desire that those who are linked by the ties of earthly kinship should be united also in fellowship with the larger family of God's people, but because souls are born individually into God's family it sometimes happens that parents are not united in surrender to God. And oftentimes children drift away from the spiritual loyalties inculcated by their parents in early years.

In such sad circumstances it may be remembered that even the family of Jesus was broken by the prejudices and jealousy of His brethren. And when heart-breaking decisions have to be made between duty to God and to those near and dear to us, there is consolation and strength in the realization that Jesus was torn by the same conflicting emotions.

Jesus warned that so far would some families according to the flesh be separated by the claims of the Gospel that "brother" would "betray brother to death, and the father the son; and children shall rise up against their parents, and shall cause them to be put to death."

This prophecy was only too tragically fulfilled during the pagan persecutions of the early centuries, and in the dark days of the Middle Ages when the apostate church of Rome sought to extinguish the faith of those who were seeking to worship God according to the dictates of their conscience.

It has been fulfilled also in more modern days when heathenism has opposed the spread of the Gospel and where the atheistic ideology of Communism has tried in vain to blot out the name and faith of Christ.

In the closing days of history we are told that Satan, knowing that his time is short, will make a final effort to divide families against themselves and against God. But the very last verses of the Old Testament contain a wonderful promise that God will be active too, seeking to reclaim the prodigal sons and daughters and prodigal fathers and mothers and bring them back into the family circle of the people of God in preparation for the day when Jesus will return.

"I will send you Elijah the prophet," He declares, "before the coming of the great and dreadful day of the Lord . . . and he shall turn the heart of the fathers to the children, and the heart of the children to their fathers."

And just as the broken family of Jesus was brought together again by the crisis of Calvary, many families now spiritually broken will be reunited in loyalty to God and belief in His Son by the catastrophic events of the last crisis of history.

The apostle Paul ends his description of the blessing of participation in the family of God with the promise: "And if children, then heirs; heirs of God, and joint heirs with Christ." In the day when Jesus comes, the children of God will enter into their glorious inheritance. What a day that will be when all who have fallen asleep in faith awake in the resurrection, and the whole family of God in heaven and earth are gathered together around His throne!

That will be the grandest reunion that has ever been!

This chapter is based on Matthew 12:46-50; Mark 3:31-35; Luke 8:19-21.

CHAPTER
FORTY-SEVEN

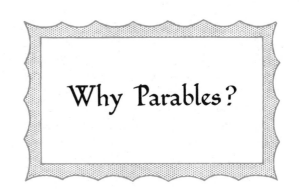

Why Parables?

WHEN Jesus was not itinerating among the cities and villages of Palestine He always stayed at the home of Peter in Capernaum. Frequently He sat in the courtyard and talked with those who came to Him, but when the crowds became too big He would go down to the shores of the Sea of Galilee and teach there.

His fishermen disciples had hired out their boats to friends, but they could always get one when Jesus needed it, for no fishing was done in the day-time and the boats were all pulled up onto the beach or riding at anchor close to the shore.

At His request they would push one of them just a little way into the water and Jesus, taking His seat in the prow, would talk to the people gathered on the beach. One of these occasions of lakeside ministry followed the visit of Mary and His brethren. It may even have been the news of the arrival of His family from Nazareth that brought together an unusually large concourse of people and necessitated Jesus' going down to the seashore.

As He seated Himself in one of the gently rocking boats the scene upon which Jesus looked was of surpassing beauty. Beyond the crowd which thronged the beach, the ripening corn on the plain of Gennesaret was a sea of rippling gold. Beyond the fields of grain, the grass-covered hill slopes were bright with red anemones, golden buttercups, and other flowers of many hues. Here and there little copses of trees provided shade and shelter for the cattle and sheep which roamed the hillsides. Birds of brilliant plumage circled in the sunshine above the fields and pastures or darted out over the lake, while waterfowl paddled about in the calm waters of the bay.

Along the shore, fishermen could be seen drying and mending their nets ready for the next night's fishing.

From a boat lying just off the shore of the lake, Jesus taught many of His fascinating parables.
By AXEL HOU   53

In His earlier ministry Jesus had often drawn lessons from the lilies of the field, the birds of the air, and other familiar sights of country, town, and lakeside; but from the autumn of the second year of His ministry He began to make a still larger use of this form of teaching in the wonderful parables which are scattered like precious gems through the later Gospel narrative.

The people who came to listen to Jesus were not unfamiliar with religious parables, for the rabbis frequently used figurative language in their teaching; but the stories Jesus told were incomparably more beautiful and vivid than the complicated parables of the rabbis, and the multitudes listened to them with rapt attention.

The disciples, however, were struck by the fact that after each story Jesus would say, "If any man have ears to hear, let him hear," or "Take heed, therefore, how ye hear," and they began to realize that there was more in the parables Jesus told than the listening crowds appreciated. So they said to Jesus: "Why speakest Thou unto them in parables?"

Jesus' answer confirmed the feeling they had about these fascinating stories. "Because," He replied, "it is given unto you to know the mysteries of the kingdom of heaven, but to them it is not given."

On the face of it the parables were simplicity itself. He spoke of sowing the fields and reaping the harvest, of fishing in the lake, of buying and selling in the market place, of domestic tasks like baking bread, and other commonplaces of daily life. The people enjoyed the stories and understood the obvious spiritual lessons they taught. But the profounder truths, the "mysteries" or "secrets" of the kingdom which they enfolded, were hidden from their unperceiving minds. Only to the disciples were these explained after the people had gone away.

In His Sermon on the Mount, Jesus had warned His disciples: "Give not that which is holy to the dogs, neither cast ye your pearls before swine, lest they trample them under their feet, and turn again and rend you." Now, as opposition from the priests, scribes, and other religious rulers grew, Jesus turned to the parabolic method of teaching in order to withhold the deeper truths of the Gospel from those who would only despise them, while in private, He revealed its "mysteries" to the receptive in heart. In doing this Jesus fulfilled yet 'another prophecy concerning Himself: "I will open My mouth in parables; I will utter things which have been kept secret from the foundation of the world."

To those who believed, Jesus said to His disciples, there "shall be given" deeper understanding of the things of God, but from those who reject My words "shall be taken away" even the knowledge they think they have. "Therefore speak I to them in parables: because they seeing see not; and hearing they hear not, neither do they understand."

"In them," He continued, "is fulfilled the prophecy of Esaias, which saith, By hearing ye shall hear, and shall not understand; and seeing ye shall see, and shall not perceive: for this people's heart is waxed gross and their ears are dull of hearing, and their eyes they have closed; lest at any time they should see with their eyes, and hear with their ears, and should understand with their heart, and should be converted, and I should heal them."

So the parables which Jesus related from this time on served two purposes. They taught simple yet beautiful lessons which delighted the multitudes. They also enshrined profound spiritual teaching about the kingdom which the disciples needed to know, so that when Jesus left them they could effectively continue the work which He had begun.

From this time in His ministry Jesus spoke "many parables," of which nearly thirty are recorded in the Gospel narratives. These fall into three distinct groups. The first seven He related by the lakeshore near Capernaum on this and succeeding days.

Under the similitudes of the sower and the seed, the wheat and tares, the mustard seed, leaven, the hidden treasure, the precious pearl, and the drag-net He told of the varied reactions of men to the Gospel, the manner of its extension into all the world, the opposition of Satan to the redemptive purpose of God, and the final separation between the righteous and the wicked in the day of judgment.

The second group of parables, following the transfiguration of Jesus, included stories like the fruitless fig tree, the great supper, the rich man and Lazarus, the Pharisee and the publican, the lost sheep, the lost coin, and the prodigal son. These foreshadowed the rejection of the self-righteous Jews and the gathering of the true Israel of God.

Finally, as Calvary loomed darkly ahead, Jesus set forth in His last prophetic parables, including the wise and foolish virgins, the wicked husbandmen, and the sheep and the goats, the vital need of preparation to meet Jesus at His coming, the blessed reward of the righteous, and the fearful fate of those who reject the Gospel of God's grace.

"Verily, I say unto you," Jesus declared to His disciples, "That many prophets and righteous men have desired to see those things which ye see, and have not seen them; and to hear these things which ye hear, and have not heard them." Then He added, "Blessed are your eyes, for they see: and your ears, for they hear."

Blessed, too, are the eyes that see, the ears that hear, and the hearts that understand today from the parables of Jesus the things which belong to their eternal peace.

This chapter is based on Matthew 13:10-17.

A Sower Goes Forth

AMONG the crowds which thronged the lakeside to listen to Jesus there must have been a very large number from the nearby villages who gained their livelihood cultivating the luxuriant soil of the almost tropical plain of Gennesaret. How their faces would light up with interest and expectancy when Jesus began the first of His fascinating parables: "Behold, a sower went forth to sow." Often He had watched the farmers at work as He crossed the fields in the springtime with His disciples. Following in the wake of the plough the sower would walk, with a sack of grain suspended at waist level from his shoulders, scattering handfuls of seed at every step. As he came near to the bridle path which crossed the field to the village, some of the seed would fall upon the earth trodden hard by man and beast. As soon as he had passed on to a safe distance, down would swoop the gulls and other birds which circled over the ploughed land, and in a few minutes every grain would be snatched up and eaten.

The eager listeners nodded their heads as Jesus said of the seeds which fell by the wayside, "the fowls came and devoured them up," for they used to say that, of three bushels of seed, one was lost to the birds, one to mice and insects, and from the remaining third they reaped their reward.

Here and there in the fields rocky outcrops of grey limestone rose up like islands above the general level. The ploughman kept well away from these, for he knew the soil around was thin and he might easily break the blade of his plough as the oxen dragged it along. So it remained untilled and barren save for the thistles and thorn scrub which sprang up wherever there was enough earth for their roots.

As the sower passed by these "stony places" some of his seed might accidentally fall upon the scanty soil or among the scattered thorn scrub. This wasted seed also had its spiritual lessons. "Some fell upon stony places," Jesus said, "where they had

---

In the parable of the sower, Jesus told of the sowing of the Gospel seed in the hearts of men.
By W. MORGAN

not much earth: and forthwith they sprung up, because they had no deepness of earth: and when the sun was up, they were scorched; and because they had no root, they withered away."

The seed which fell among the thorny undergrowth had a rather different fate. In the deeper earth it grew and even gave promise of fruit at harvest time. But, alas, the thorns sprang up even faster "and choked" the struggling grain before it could reach maturity.

But the labour of the sower was by no means all in vain. The greater part of the seed fell into the deep, freshly turned loam. There it germinated and, helped by the early rains and the warm sun, it soon covered the fields with a forest of springing green blades. With the coming of summer, tall green stalks emerged which bent under the weight of the ears by which they were crowned. Gradually, the ears fattened and turned from green to gold. At last "the full corn in the ear" was ready for the sickle and the ploughmen and sowers went forth to gather in the ripened grain.

This thrilling climax to the toil of spring and summer brought Jesus' parable to its close. "But other fell into good ground," He said, "and brought forth fruit, some an hundredfold, some sixtyfold, and some thirtyfold."

The listening farmers smiled in recollection of the fortunate years when they received as much as an hundredfold for their labours. Then they not only had enough for their own needs till the next harvest, but also a surplus to sell to the Roman authorities for the provisioning of the legions out on the Syrian frontiers of the empire. They remembered other years which were not so good, when their grain produced only sixtyfold or thirty, but even so they were thankful.

Certainly Jesus understood the vicissitudes of the farmer's life and their hearts were drawn to this sympathetic Teacher. They took to heart, too, the implied question of His parable: What kind of soil did their hearts provide for the spiritual seed He sowed? But they did not explore its deeper meaning.

When later Jesus was talking with His disciples alone He reverted to the subject of the parable and began to show them how accurately its details had been fulfilled in His ministry. "Hear ye therefore the parable of the sower," Jesus began. The seed, He explained, was the living "Word of the kingdom" and He Himself was the divine Sower. He had not come, as so many imagined, to lead the Jews to battle against their Roman overlords and to give them back their national independence. He had come to sow the grain of divine truth from which a spiritual harvest would spring forth. "He that heareth My word, and believeth on Him that sent Me, hath everlasting life."

The field, to begin with, was Israel, but as the sowers of Gennesaret often had to go long distances to far-away fields, the Gospel sowers would ere long be "sent forth" into all the world.

The soil into which the precious seed fell was human hearts. The rain was the gentle dew of the Spirit and the warm sun the outpouring of God's love.

Sad to say, the words of Jesus often fell upon hearts as impenetrable as the hard-trodden paths across the cornfields. "When any one heareth the Word of the kingdom, and understandeth it not," He said, "then cometh the wicked one, and catcheth away that which was sown in his heart. This is he which received seed by the wayside."

The proud scribes and Pharisees, the worldly-minded Sadducees, the ambitious and office-seeking Herodians, were examples of the hard ground into which the Gospel seed could find no entrance. At times some word of Jesus did penetrate, as it were, a crack in the self-righteous front which they presented and they began to feel embarrassed and uncomfortable. But before the seed could become embedded it was snatched quickly away by the ever-watchful "prince of the power of the air," and was lost.

And such, all too often, is the fate of the Word in our secularized and pleasure-crazed age. So many hearts today are hardened past feeling or too careless and indifferent to surrender a moment from the things of time and sense to consider the paramount questions of moral responsibility and eternal destiny. And if perchance such are arrested in the pursuit of wealth and power and pleasure by some disturbing event, or challenging happening, more often than not the thoughts are diverted quickly into other channels by the enemy of souls and the precious Seed is snatched unavailingly away.

Then, continued Jesus, there is the seed which falls into stony ground. "He that received the seed into stony places, the same is he that heareth the word, and anon with joy receiveth it." This was typical of the multitude of common people who heard Jesus "gladly." Their hearts responded to His sympathy and were gripped by the power of His words, so different from the platitudes of the scribes and teachers of the law. And the Word of the kingdom quickly germinated in their hearts.

But, went on Jesus, such ones have no root in themselves, and though they endure for a while, "when tribulation or persecution ariseth because of the Word," they are "offended."

Many of the people who listened to Jesus believed that He was about to declare Himself the King of the Jews. They hoped that soon He would deliver them from their trials and oppression under the Romans and that the blessing of God would return to Israel.

But when they heard Him tell one would-be follower that He had nowhere to lay His head, they began to realize that to follow Jesus meant even more hardship and tribulation than they were at present experiencing, and they could not face it. They were "offended" and "walked no more with Him." Some later were among those who cried, "Crucify Him."

Such are like many in our day who impulsively surrender themselves to Christ through some sudden spiritual experience, such as a great revival campaign. Like the common people in Jesus' day they receive the Word with gladness of heart and passionately pledge themselves to follow the Master. But when they discover that the Christian life is not always smooth and easy, but is a daily battle against seen and unseen forces of wickedness, the unhealthy forced growth of a superficial experience is withered ere it is finally rooted, and they slip back into the darkness.

It is not enough initially to accept Jesus. We must count the cost of discipleship, for "we are made partakers of Christ" only "if we hold the beginning of our confidence steadfast unto the end." "He that shall endure unto the end, the same shall be saved."

The man "that receiveth seed among the thorns," went on Jesus, is he "that heareth the Word" and in whose heart it germinates, giving promise of a bountiful harvest. But, sad to say, the thorns of "care" and "the deceitfulness of riches," spring up around the spiritual root faster than it can grow, taking away its nourishment, shutting out the light and air from above, and so choking the Word and preventing it reaching maturity. There were no fewer than twenty-two varieties of prickly plants among the thorn scrub of Palestine, and there is just as long a list of spiritual "thorns" which menace the delicate plants of Christian growth if they are permitted to encumber our lives.

In His Sermon on the Mount, Jesus declared that it is impossible to serve God and cling to the world, and in this parable He underlines again the exclusiveness of the Gospel call. No rank growth of harassing care or noxious weeds of inordinate desire or ambition, no cankering pleasures must be allowed to crowd in and stifle spiritual development. No snare of earthly treasure or lust of other things must be permitted to lure the affections of the heart away from the riches of divine grace. How many a modern rich young ruler, or Demas, has "loved this present world" and been lost to the kingdom? How many, like Judas, have even grievously betrayed the church of God for the gain of gold?

No wonder the Scriptures so insistently urge the children of God to mind not "earthly things" nor to be "overcharged with surfeiting, and drunkenness," lest the reaping time come and find them empty ears, having an appearance of godliness, but devoid of its reality and power.

Only, concluded Jesus, when the soil of the heart is ploughed by conviction into a deep and fertile loam, cleansed of the weeds of sin, and made soft and receptive by the gentle rain of the Spirit can the Word of the kingdom find safe and permanent lodgement.

But when it falls into such good and honest soil like that of the Thessalonians who received the preaching of Paul "not as the word of men, but as it is in truth, the Word of God," it will germinate and silently develop by the mysterious power of the Spirit from blade to ear, and at last to the maturity of the "full corn in the ear" of a noble life. "For as the earth bringeth forth her bud, and as the garden causeth the things that are sown in it to spring forth; so the Lord God will cause righteousness and praise to spring forth."

The harvest may, under God, be an hundredfold, as in a Peter or a Paul, or it may be only the thirtyfold of some humble disciple; but if there is fruitage according to the gifts God has given, it brings equal joy to the heart of God and rejoicing in heaven.

This chapter is based on Matthew 13:1-9, 18-23; Mark 4:1-9, 14-20; Luke 8:4-8, 11-15

Tares Among the Wheat

SOON after Jesus related His first fascinating parable of the sower, or rather of the soils, to the crowds gathered by the lakeside, He had another story for them. This also was one about the farmer and his fields, but it introduced a new feature which at once caught the interest of the listening multitude.

"The kingdom of heaven," began Jesus, "is likened unto a man which sowed good seed in his field: but while men slept, his enemy came and sowed tares among the wheat, and went his way." And so, in due course, "when the blade was sprung up . . . . then appeared the tares also."

The farmers in the crowd knew well enough the trouble that weeds could be in their wheat fields. Particularly they feared the bearded darnel, or poisonous rye grass, whose seeds, if they got among the grain, could cause nausea, convulsions, and even death. Couch grass, or "creeping wheat," was another source of vexation, for its roots spread out under the soil and became inextricably entangled with the roots of the wheat stalks, making removal quite impossible. So the husbandman took every precaution to make sure that the seed he used was uncontaminated by any of these weeds.

Naturally, therefore, the servants of the husbandman in Jesus' story were very surprised at the appearance of tares among the wheat and they at once went to their master with the question: "Sir, didst thou not sow good seed in this field? from whence then hath it tares?" And to their consternation he replied, "An enemy hath done this."

It was bad enough when the tares sprang up in the fields as a result of seed blown by the winds, but it was a dastardly thing for a vindictive farmer to come by night and deliberately sow tares in his neighbour's field.

61

The people were now tensely listening to hear how Jesus would deal with this serious situation in His story. He went on: "The servants said unto him, Wilt thou then that we go and gather them up?"

The farmers smiled incredulously. They knew how impossible a task this would be. And so did the husbandman in the parable. "Nay," he said to his servants; "lest while ye gather up the tares, ye root up also the wheat with them. Let both grow together until the harvest: and in the time of the harvest I will say to the reapers, Gather ye together first the tares, and bind them in bundles to burn them: but gather the wheat into my barn."

There were general nods of approval at this method of dealing with the tares. Jesus certainly knew more about farming than they had imagined.

But what was the lesson that they were to learn from it? This was a more difficult parable than His first one about the different soils, and they were perplexed.

The disciples also were at a loss to understand its meaning and so, as soon as they got back to Jesus' lodging they asked Him: "Declare unto us the parable of the tares of the field," and readily Jesus began to explain.

This second parable of the kingdom revealed the hatred of Satan to the work of the Gospel and foreshadowed the history of the church in the world from the apostles' day until the time when Christ's kingdom would be established. It was in many ways to be a sad story, but it would have a triumphant ending.

"He that soweth the good seed," said Jesus, "is the Son of man." "The field," in which the seed is sown, "is the world." Thus again Jesus pointed beyond His present ministry to the "house of Israel' to the time when the Gospel should go "to every nation, and kindred, and tongue, and people."

"The good seed," or rather the fruitage from it, Jesus went on, represents "the children of the kingdom," the tares are "the children of the wicked one," and the enemy that sowed them is "the devil."

In this vivid picture Jesus revealed that Satan would not only harden the hearts of many so that the Gospel seed could find no lodgement in them, but he would also introduce into the church many having the appearance of "children of the kingdom," just as tares resemble wheat, but who were really "children of the wicked one." Working for Satan from inside the church they would seek to corrupt its purity, disrupt its fellowship, and bring dishonour upon its fair name.

How true all this has proved in the story of the Christian church. Into the company of the disciples Judas intruded himself, and in the lifetime of the first apostles they had to warn of "false teachers" bringing in "damnable heresies, even denying the Lord that bought them," of "grievous wolves" entering in "not sparing the flock," of "false prophets, deceitful workers, transforming themselves into the apostles of Christ."

As we read the record of subsequent centuries we are shocked to discover how successful the "enemy" was in introducing the false teachings of image worship, Mary worship, the invocation of saints, the superstitious use of relics, prayers for the dead, meritorious works, penances, etc., until the "faith which was once delivered unto the saints" was almost obscured beneath an accretion of false teachings and sinful practices.

So far did the corruption of the primitive teaching of the Gospel go that the church which should have been "the mystery of godliness" came to be dominated by "the mystery of iniquity" in the form of the papal church of the Dark Ages.

In the great Reformation movement the church freed itself to a large extent from the shackles of papal apostasy, but, sad to relate, Satan soon began to make new sowings of the tares of scepticism, modernism, evolutionary teaching, etc., as well as reseeding the Romanist tares, which have spread so rapidly that, as the prophetic Word forewarned, there is again far more of the "form of godliness" in the church than there is of its reality and power. The tares once more are thick among the wheat!

Many people must wonder why has God permitted these fearful perversions of the Gospel to persist in the church. This parable is the answer. It is the answer also to such perplexing questions as why Jesus retained Judas in the company of the disciples and why God did not stop Satan's evil work of corrupting the angels in heaven before sin entered our world.

In the providence of God, Satan's tares of disloyalty were allowed to grow in heaven in order that their poisonous fruit might be manifest to all the angel hosts. Jesus did not expose Judas until his treachery was manifest. And for the same reason God will permit the tares which Satan has sown in the church to reach their evil maturity in order that the final contrast between "the mystery of godliness" and "the mystery of iniquity" may be as clear as between wheat and tares.

During the centuries there have been those who, contrary to the counsel of Jesus in His parable, have presumed to pull up by the violence of persecution what they alleged to be tares. By their cruel deeds, however, they have revealed themselves not as the obedient servants of the divine husbandmen but "children of the wicked one." And while professing to be rooting out tares they have actually sought to destroy the true wheat.

In the terrible persecutions and massacres of the Dark Ages the prelates of the Roman church were the very instruments of Satan, while the Waldenses, the Huguenots, and other Protestants whom they persecuted were the true "children of the kingdom." What a warning these fearful deeds are to those who, in the church of God today, may be tempted to arrogate to themselves the right to judge their fellow-men.

But despite the attempts of the enemy to destroy the "wheat" and multiply the

Plates On Next Two Pages: Page 64. A farmer sows his seed in modern Palestine. Page 65. Thorns and thistles may be very alluring, but they choke the growing seed. So, said Jesus, do the sinful pleasures of the world.

"tares," the work of God has spread from land to land, until today the field encompasses the whole earth.

True to the word of Jesus the church in the world still comprises both the true "children of the kingdom" and the "children of the evil one" and by no means all the names upon the church rolls on earth are registered in heaven.

Sometimes those of the world point to members of the church and accuse them of hypocrisy, of not living up to their profession. Often this is only too true. But far from condemning the church, these unworthy ones are an evidence of the long-suffering of God for, in the spiritual sense, though not in nature, it is always possible for the tares to become good wheat. This is an additional reason why men should not attempt the work of separation before the harvest. For if it is wellnigh impossible for human wisdom to discern which is which now, even less is it possible to discern which shall be wheat and which tares when the reaping time comes.

This does not, of course, mean that false doctrines and sinful actions should not be exposed. The Word of God has been given, as Paul tells us, for "doctrine, for reproof, for correction, for instruction in righteousness: that the man of God may be perfect, throughly furnished unto all good works." It is therefore to be faithfully preached "in season and out of season," to those who know it not and also to those who are failing to fully maintain the "faith" and to keep all "the commandments of God." But ultimate judgment must be left to God and to the harvest time when Jesus will come to effect the final separation.

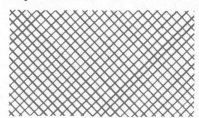

Jesus used the growing corn to illustrate the fruitage of the good seed of the Gospel in human hearts.

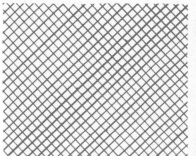

In that day, when the angels go forth at His command, no false claims will deceive them, for their separation will not be according to human judgment, but by the records in the books of heaven. Unhesitatingly the angels will "discern between the righteous and the wicked, between him that serveth God and him that serveth Him not."

"Then," says Jesus, "shall the righteous shine forth." Because man does not see as God sees there have been those in the church who have "shone" in the world's eyes, yet whose light will go out in obscurity in the final assessment. On the other hand, there are saints of God who have lived and died unheralded and unsung, who will "shine forth" when their true worth is manifest in His kingdom.

How wise then is the inspired counsel of the apostle Peter: "Give diligence to make your calling and election sure," that when Jesus comes you may not be among the "bundles" gathered by the angels to be burned, but among the wheat that is safely garnered into the heavenly barn.

This chapter is based on Matthew 13:24-30, 36-43.

CHAPTER FIFTY

The Mustard Seed and the Leaven

THE disciples of Jesus were greatly distressed by the growing enmity of the scribes and Pharisees, and when Jesus warned them that the enemies of the Gospel would multiply within the church as "tares of the field," they began to wonder what hope there was of the success of Jesus' mission and the establishment of His kingdom. It was to dispel their evident discouragement that in His next two parables Jesus highlighted the ultimate triumph of the Gospel.

Said Jesus: "The kingdom of heaven is like to a grain of mustard seed, which a man took, and sowed in his field: which indeed is the least of all seeds: but when it is grown, it is the greatest among herbs, and becometh a tree, so that the birds of the air come and lodge in the branches thereof."

There were at least two varieties of mustard which flourished in Palestine in Jesus' day and their abundance by the shores of Galilee doubtless led Him to choose this plant as the subject of a parable.

Because the mustard seed was the smallest with which the Jews were familiar, it was proverbially used to signify anything very small. "As small as a mustard seed," people would say. Yet considering its smallness, the bush into which it grew was surprisingly large. Of course, the mustard tree did not bear comparison with the giant oak or the cedar of Lebanon, but judged by other "herbs" its growth was remarkable. Travellers have reported seeing mustard trees in the fertile Plain of Acre as tall as a man on horseback, while down in the tropical valley of the Jordan they grow even higher. Goldfinches and linnets seem to have a particular liking for mustard trees and are often seen fluttering around and even nesting upon their ample branches.

What a picture this provides of the humble beginnings yet mighty expansion of God's kingdom of grace. "A virgin shall conceive, and bear a Son," wrote the Gospel

---

As leaven silently permeates the whole lump of dough, so the Gospel works from within, renewing mind and heart and transforming the life.

prophet Isaiah. "Ye shall find the Babe wrapped in swaddling clothes, lying in a manger," the angel told the shepherds in the fields of Bethlehem on the night Jesus was born. It was a humble entrance into the world for Him who was to be called "Wonderful, Counsellor, The mighty God, The everlasting Father, The Prince of Peace." And the first thirty years of His life as a peasant Carpenter in a mountain village in Galilee gave little indication that one day "the government" would be upon "His shoulder" and that of the "increase of His government" there would be "no end."

The twelve men whom Jesus chose as His first disciples were an undistinguished group, untravelled, mostly uneducated, and with few resources. No-one but Jesus would have appointed such as His heralds nor would anyone else have chosen as His headquarters a dingy upper room in a narrow street of old Jerusalem.

Yet the divine seed planted in the tiny "field" of Palestine in a forgotten corner of the world-embracing empire of Rome, miraculously grew, and within a few centuries became a mighty tree. Since then, despite apostasy within and opposition from without it has continued to grow until today it encompasses the earth. As far into the icy wastes around the poles as men dwell, the Gospel has gone. It has penetrated the remotest oases of the deserts, the thickest jungles, far up into the highest mountains, and across the wide seas to distant isles, as well as into the cities and villages of civilized lands, till almost all men everywhere have had the opportunity of hearing and responding to the Gospel call. And today the message is speeding on its way by land, sea, and air to the last frontiers of mankind.

Soon, as God has declared, it will have gone to "every nation, and kindred, and tongue, and people," the earth will have been "lightened with His glory," and His people will be ready and waiting to receive their coming King.

If the farmers who listened to Jesus appreciated the lesson of the mighty power within a tiny seed, the housewives who had joined the crowd from town and village must have become very interested when Jesus began to talk about leaven.

"The kingdom of heaven," He said, as He began another parable, "is like unto leaven, which a woman took and hid in three measures of meal, till the whole was leavened."

Three measures or an ephah of meal was about the quantity which a Jewish housewife would normally take to prepare bread for her household. When the three visitors came to Abraham's tent in the plain of Mamre, Sarah took "three measures of fine meal" to "make cakes upon the hearth" for them.

Into her bowl of meal the housewife would mix an appropriate quantity of leaven, together with water enough to make a dough. After kneading, she would set it aside to rise under the invisible influence of the leaven till it filled the kneading trough and even began to pour over the sides.

In the Scriptures the action of leaven is mostly used as a symbol of the permeating power of sin. For this reason it was scrupulously excluded from the offerings used in the temple sacrifices and from all food eaten during the Passover season. Jesus Himself referred to the "leaven of the Pharisees," and Paul speaks of the "leaven

of malice and wickedness." But in the parable of the leaven it illustrates the operation of grace in the human heart and the manner of growth of God's kingdom in
the world.

In contrast with the veneer of outward conformity imposed by the Pharisees, the
Gospel leaven "hid" in the lives of men would work silently from within, transforming the heart, renewing the mind, purifying the thoughts, purging the conscience,
sanctifying the desires, until the "old man" was no more, and there emerged a "new
creature," fashioned after the divine similitude in Christ Jesus. As the apostle Paul
so vividly describes the process in his epistle to the Romans: "For what the law
could not do, in that it was weak through the flesh, God sending His own Son in
the likeness of sinful flesh, and for sin, condemned sin in the flesh: that the righteousness of the law might be fulfilled in us, who walk not after the flesh, but after the
Spirit."

The kingdom of God was not to be spectacularly imposed upon men by a warrior
Messiah, as was the common belief of the Jews. It would be extended, not by force
of arms but by the power of love, not by outward might but by the hidden forces
of the Spirit. Transcending the barriers of race, nation, and class, the leaven of the
Gospel would spread in the hearts of men until the "whole lump" of humankind
was leavened.

Today the Gospel leaven has nearly completed its work in the lives of men and
the tree of grace has almost reached its full development. Soon Jesus will return to
transform the "hidden" kingdom of grace into the visible kingdom of glory which
shall extend to the ends of the earth and endure for ever.

This chapter is based on Matthew 13:31-33; Mark 4:30-32; Luke 13:18-21.

God's Treasure Trove

IN His earlier parables of the kingdom, Jesus drew His illustrations from the culti-
vation of the soil and from the domestic life of the Jewish home. But in the
crowds who followed Him there must also have been many merchants and traders
passing through Capernaum on business. No doubt Jesus had such in mind when He
began to tell more of His fascinating stories.

"Again," He said, "the kingdom of heaven is like unto treasure hid in a field;
the which when a man hath found, he hideth, and for joy thereof goeth and selleth
all that he hath, and buyeth that field."

Such incidents as this were by no means uncommon in ancient times when there
were no strong rooms, banks, or safe deposits. In those days the only way to secure
treasure against theft by robbers and looting in time of war, was to bury it. To keep
secret the place of concealment a man might not even tell those of his own household and if perchance he was killed or died suddenly all knowledge of the where-
abouts of the treasure might be lost.

In his parable Jesus told of a tenant-farmer who was one day ploughing the
field he rented when his plough or harrow struck a box of treasure which had been
buried there and forgotten.

Without telling anyone of his discovery he carefully covered up the hoard and
began negotiations for the purchase of the field, for, according to Jewish law, buried
treasure belonged to the owner of the ground in which it was found.

He was only a poor man and he had to sell everything to raise the money,
but he managed it and purchased the field. As soon as it was his he hurried back
and dug up the treasure. His fortunes were immediately more than restored, for, in
return for his poor possessions, he had gained undreamed-of riches.

When Jesus had finished this story He went on to tell another about a dealer in pearls. Capernaum was on one of the great trade routes between the East and the Mediterranean world, and over the desert, by way of Damascus, came camel caravans laden with treasures of the Orient, pearls from tropical seas, precious stones, silks, spices, and amber. There may actually have been a trader in pearls among the crowd when Jesus declared: "The kingdom of heaven is like unto a merchant man, seeking goodly pearls: who, when he had found one pearl of great price, went and sold all that he had, and bought it."

In these two parables the "treasure" and the "pearl of great price" fitly represent Christ through whom the precious gift of salvation comes to us. The apostle Paul truly says of Him, "In whom are hid all the treasures of wisdom and knowledge." In Him, too, are all treasures of grace and glory. No wonder Peter speaks of the "precious promises" of God and says of Jesus, "Unto you therefore which believe He is precious."

Just as the good fortune of acquiring earthly treasure came to the tenant-farmer and the pearl dealer, so, in God's providence, the opportunity of salvation comes to each one. But as the two stories suggest, it may come to different individuals in different ways.

In the first story the buried treasure was found quite accidentally. This is illustrative of the many souls who literally stumble upon the Gospel before a realization of its worth dawns upon them.

Through the ages Satan has sought to cover up and hide away from man a knowledge of the goodness of God and the riches of His grace in order that he may encompass mankind in his own ruin. As the apostle Paul explains, "If our Gospel be hid, it is hid to them that are lost: in whom the god of this world hath blinded the minds of them which believe not, lest the light of the glorious Gospel of Christ, who is the image of God, should shine unto them."

Some, Satan has blinded by the crudest idolatries, others by finespun yet vain philosophy and intellectual conceit; some, by gross materialism and sensuality, others by a formal and powerless religion like that of the Jews in Jesus' day. The measure of Satan's success is evident in the countless multitudes who live out their lives unconscious of the spiritual treasures within their reach and only waiting to be grasped.

But in His love and mercy God seeks to uncover what Satan has hidden. As the farmer, working away in his field quite unexpectedly ran his plough into the buried box of treasure, so by His mysterious providences, God leads souls dead to spiritual things suddenly to glimpse the hidden treasures of divine love. It may be by an apparently chance meeting with some godly saint, through a tract picked up in a bus, by an invitation to an evangelistic service, the sight of some deed of Christian heroism in time of mortal danger, or through sudden affliction or adversity. All too often the priceless opportunity is unrecognized and dismissed. The world pulls too hard or preconceived opinions and prejudices are too strongly entrenched, and darkness again settles upon the mind. But some, like Paul when he was confronted by

Christ on the Damascus road, are not "disobedient unto the heavenly vision." They stop to investigate, they begin to dig, and they find the heavenly treasure. It is of such that God speaks when He says, "I am found of them that sought Me not."

On the other hand, there are many who are deeply conscious of an unsatisfied spiritual need in their lives and who, like the merchantman, devote themselves to a diligent search for the pearl of "great price."

The wise men from the East, Cornelius the Roman centurion, and the Ethiopian eunuch were typical of many among the heathen nations in Jesus' day who were seeking for the true God. Among the Jews were many, dissatisfied with the self-righteousness, the empty ceremonial and traditionalism of the Pharisees, who went out into the wilderness to hear John the Baptist and later joined the crowds who followed Jesus. And when the Gospel was spread abroad by Paul and the other apostles, multitudes among the Gentiles "turned to God from idols to serve the living and true God; and to wait for His Son from heaven."

In our day also there are many who, conscious of the emptiness of their lives, are turning from the baubles of earthly riches, honour, and power and from the spurious pearls of formal religion to seek rest of soul in true fellowship with God and a knowledge of His truth. These are proving, as so many have done in bygone days, the surety of the promise, "Seek, and ye shall find."

But whether men are confronted suddenly with the challenge of the Gospel or find the truth through long and diligent search, possession of the treasure demands the surrender of all else. As both the tenant-farmer and the merchant had to sell all to acquire the prize, the soul that would win Christ and His salvation must count all else but loss. God will not confide His treasure to a heart which still cherishes unholy ambitions and worldly desires. He will not share a human heart with Satan. Sin must be dethroned if grace is to reign.

Neither of the men in the parable questioned the price they had to pay, because they knew that their reward would far outweigh the sacrifice. The farmer "for joy thereof" sold everything he had. The treasure was cheap at the price! Similarly, the disciples "left all" to follow Jesus. When Paul sensed his need of Christ he cast away his pride, his position, and his prosperity as "dung" that he might lay hold of the "prize of the high calling of God in Christ Jesus." And if we truly esteem the "exceeding riches of His grace," no earthly possession, opportunity, ambition, or prospect, will be worth holding on to.

If this price seems too high, as it did to the rich young ruler who came to Jesus, it is because the true worth of God's salvation is not realized. When a man is convinced that it is a treasure beyond all else, any sacrifice will be dwarfed by comparison.

It may perhaps be thought that there is a contradiction between the appeal of God through the prophet Isaiah, "Ho, every one that thirsteth, come ye to the waters, and he that hath no money; come ye, buy . . . wine and milk without money and without price," and these two parables in which the farmer and the merchant had to sacrifice all in order to possess themselves of the treasure. In the book of Revelation also we read the invitation to the Laodicean church, "I counsel thee to buy of Me gold tried in the fire, that thou mayest be rich."

There is, however, no contradiction. Salvation certainly cannot be bought like an earthly commodity, as Simon Magus found to his cost. Paul makes it very clear that it is "by grace" that we are "saved through faith." It is, he declares, "not of yourselves; it is the gift of God." Elsewhere he emphasizes that salvation is a "free gift."

But, at the same time, it can be received only by those who abandon themselves to Christ. We ourselves are the price He asks. Salvation costs all that there is of us, yet our all is nothing in comparison with the gift.

A poor man can pay this price as easily as a rich man. The educated have no advantage over the ignorant. In fact, the price is often more easily paid by the poor than by the rich, by the humble more easily than by the proud. All too often those who have every earthly advantage imagine that they are "rich, and increased with goods, and have need of nothing." So, as Jesus said to the Pharisees, "The publicans and the harlots go into the kingdom of God before you."

Wonderful indeed is this transaction of grace whereby, in return for the surrender of our poor selves, we receive the "unspeakable gift" of redemption in Christ. And yet even that is only the beginning of the heavenly bounty. For, as the apostle Paul tells us, "He that spared not His own Son, but delivered Him up for us all, how shall He not with Him also freely give us all things?"

Although we give up "all" to win Christ, with Him we receive again "all" that is worth while in this life as well as being "heirs" of "all things" in the world to come.

No wonder that the apostle Paul cried out in ecstasy, "The sufferings of this present time are not worthy to be compared with the glory which shall be revealed in us."

This chapter is based on Matthew 13:44-46.

The Gospel Net

ONCE again Jesus was sitting in Peter's boat by the lakeshore, with the crowd gathered on the beach in front of Him. A little distance away a group of fishermen were washing their nets and mending the holes in them ready for the next night's fishing. The scene suggested to Jesus an illustration for another of His parables.

"The kingdom of heaven," He said, "is like unto a net, that was cast into the sea, and gathered of every kind: which, when it was full, they drew to shore, and sat down, and gathered the good into vessels, but cast the bad away. So shall it be at the end of the world: the angels shall come forth, and sever the wicked from among the just, and shall cast them into the furnace of fire: there shall be wailing and gnashing of teeth."

In this parable Jesus emphasized again the truths that He had earlier taught in the parables of the sower and of the tares of the field.

There were two kinds of fishing nets used on Galilee in the days of Jesus. One was the small casting net which could be handled by a fisherman working alone or with a companion. This was used for inshore fishing.

The other was the much larger drag-net. As its name implies, it was heavily weighted so as to hang vertically and was dragged through deep water between two boats, enmeshing shoals of fish as it moved along.

While the casting net might very well symbolize the individual "fisher of men" the drag-net aptly illustrated the work of the Gospel as a whole, gathering the people of God out of the vast sea of the nations.

Sometimes when the fishermen went out with their drag-nets their haul was disappointingly small. At other times they would net great quantities of fish. Similar

---

The fishermen disciples of Jesus could well understand the meaning of His parable of the Gospel net.

is the experience of those who go forth to "catch men." Sometimes God's fishermen labour long and hard but catch "nothing." Not discouraged, however, they let down their nets again, at the Lord's bidding, to encompass a "multitude of fishes." Pentecost was one of those miraculous draughts corresponding with the "hundred-fold" increase in the parable of the sower.

Fishing with a drag-net, of course, gathered in all sorts of fish. The majority met the Levitical requirement of fins and scales and commanded a good price on the quay or in the market. Some, however, did not meet the required specifications and were not marketable.

This illustrates the different sorts and conditions of men who are gathered into the church by the Gospel net. Not all who accept the invitation of the Gospel are

---

The parable of the net well illustrates the work of the Gospel as it gathers the church of God out of the vast sea of the nations.

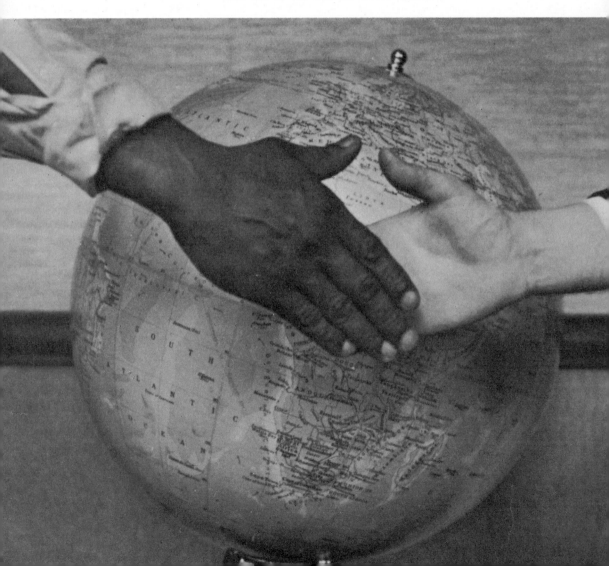

accounted "clean" by the Lord. Some associate themselves with the people of God, as Judas joined the disciple band, for material advantage. They are not really converted; they manifest a "form of godliness," but they are devoid of the power of the Spirit. Some, like Demas, vainly try to combine love to God with a love of the world. Still others, like Hymenæus and Philetus, are actually false teachers deliberately insinuated by Satan into the church to bring about confusion and dissension.

When Israel came out of Egyptian bondage they were a very "mixed multitude" and so also has the church been throughout its history. Right on until the end of time it will be comprised of wheat and tares, good fish and bad.

Nowhere does the Bible suggest that the visible church will ever be wholly pure. It warns, in fact, that in the last days there will be seen an apostasy more fearful even than that in the Dark Ages, and that only a "remnant" will be found keeping "the commandments of God, and the faith of Jesus."

In the parable of the husbandman, the wheat and the tares remained intertwined until "the harvest." In the parable of the drag-net the good and bad fish are mingled in the net until the sweep is finished and the net is hauled onto the beach. In other words, not until the Gospel has been "preached in all the world for a witness unto all nations," and the Gospel net is drawn up onto the farther shore of time can the work of separation be undertaken.

No self-appointed church has a right to cast souls out of the kingdom of God, much less to cast them into a furnace of fire as Rome did when she burned heretics at the stake.

The work of separation belongs solely to Jesus and will be carried out at "the end of the world" when He comes with His angels to execute judgment. Then the good fish will be separated from the bad, the wheat from the tares, and there will be "wailing and gnashing of teeth" as the wicked are cast into the "furnace of fire prepared" for the destruction of "the devil, and his angels" and for all who are deceived by them.

One of the solemn warnings of Jesus was that "many are called, but few are chosen," and the apostle Paul himself was concerned that, having preached the Gospel to others, he himself should not be a "castaway."

Enrolment in the records of the church on earth is no guarantee of a part with Christ in His kingdom. Such will be the privilege only of those whose names are also "written in heaven." Many in the day of separation will cry, "Lord, Lord," and He will sorrowfully say, "I never knew you."

How important it is then that we heed the counsel of the apostle Peter, "Give diligence to make your calling and election sure," for only if we do this now will an "entrance" be ministered unto us "abundantly into the everlasting kingdom of our Lord and Saviour Jesus Christ."

This chapter is based on Matthew 13:47-50.

Things New and Old

WHEN Jesus ended His parable of the drag-net He turned to His disciples and asked them, "Have ye understood all these things?"

"Yea, Lord," they replied.

The disciples had not, of course, comprehended the full significance of the parables of Jesus, but, thanks to His private explanations, they had understood all that was needful at the time. So Jesus accepted their reply without comment and went on to tell them why He had made known the great truths of the kingdom.

"Every scribe," He said, "which is instructed unto the kingdom of heaven is like unto a man that is an householder, which bringeth forth out of his treasure things new and old."

Jesus is the divine Householder and Keeper of all the "treasures" of wisdom and knowledge and grace. In His preaching and teaching He was ever exhibiting new beauties in the age-old truths which God had committed to Israel, and He purposed that the disciples instructed by Him would in turn become dispensers of "things new and old" from the treasure store of divine truth.

By designating His disciples "scribes," Jesus was contrasting them with those known by that name among the Jews but who, sad to say, had so tragically failed God and the nation.

They claimed to be the appointed instructors of Israel, yet they were actually blind to the significance of much of the "old" truth set forth in the law, the prophets, and the history of God's ancient people, and they utterly failed to recognize the "new" truth of the purpose of God in Christ. By their refusal to accept the new revelation of Jesus they revealed how little they comprehended the "old" things which God had before declared. If they had comprehended the "old" things they would have

---

Beside the Sea of Galilee Jesus unfolded to the multitudes things old and new in God's wonderful purpose of redemption. By J. J. TISSOT

recognized that the truths which Jesus declared emanated from the same divine Source.

From the very first promise of the Redeemer in Eden, the Person and work of Christ had been set forth in the Gospel declared to the patriarchs, in the types and symbols of the sanctuary and its services, in the psalms of David, and in the messages of the prophets. Every detail concerning His incarnation, His life, and His ministry had been foretold in minute detail in hundreds of prophecies, so that Jesus was able confidently to declare, "They are they which testify of Me."

The disciples learned from Jesus much concerning the wonderful fulfilment of those Old Testament types and prophecies, yet after His death and resurrection He had to chide them for failing to "believe all that the prophets" had spoken. "Ought not Christ to have suffered these things, and to enter into His glory?" He asked two of them and later, to the assembled disciples in Jerusalem, He said, "These are the words which I spake unto you, while I was yet with you, that all things must be fulfilled, which were written in the law of Moses, and in the prophets, and in the psalms concerning Me."

The disciples accepted the gentle reproof and went forth boldly to declare that Jesus, whom wicked hands had taken and crucified, was both "Christ" and "Lord." Peter was speaking for all his fellow "scribes" when he wrote, in his second epistle, "Wherefore I will not be negligent to put you always in remembrance of these things, though ye know them, and be established in the present truth."

The fate of the false scribes in the catastrophe which a few decades later overwhelmed Jerusalem and the Jewish nation is a tragic warning of the danger of neglecting "present truth." And the sterility of modern Judaism in contrast with the missionary faith of Israel of old is a fulfilment of the divine sentence, "Whosoever hath not, from him shall be taken away even that he hath."

But while the Jewish nation was destroyed because it rejected the "new" revelation of God in Christ, an equally disastrous mistake was soon to be made by many in the Christian church. For there arose teachers who set the "new" things of the Gospel in opposition to the "old" things of the covenant of Sinai. Professing to exalt the grace of God they declared that the Christian was henceforth absolved from obedience to the law. By this aberration of the Gospel, however, they revealed their ignorance of the true nature of the new revelation in Christ. Of Him prophecy had declared, "He will magnify the law, and make it honourable," and He Himself specifically asserted, "Till heaven and earth pass, one jot or one tittle shall in no wise pass from the law, till all be fulfilled."

These false teachers failed to comprehend that grace and law are complementary not antagonistic to one another, that the "righteousness of the law," cannot be attained apart from the Gospel, and that the Gospel of grace is made of none effect if it is divorced from obedience to "the commandments of God." Condemning this erroneous teaching at its inception Paul emphasized, in his epistle to the Romans, that "the righteousness of the law" is to "be fulfilled in us, who walk not after the flesh, but after the Spirit." The modern not-under-law advocates, therefore, who attempt to separate the law and the Gospel are as culpable as those whom Paul reproved. The true people of God today, as John the Revelator emphasizes, are "they that keep the commandments of God, and the faith of Jesus."

While Jesus was with His disciples He frankly told them that there were many new things which they could not "bear," particularly with reference to the trials and tribulations of the church between His ascension to heaven and His return in glory. These, however, would be progressively revealed to them by the Spirit, who would lead them into "all truth."

These revelations came to the church in the inspired letters penned by the apostles, and culminated in "the Revelation of Jesus Christ, which God gave unto Him, to show unto His servants things which must shortly come to pass," and which "He sent and signified . . . by His angel unto His servant John."

Down the centuries these "new things" of the prophetic Word have been "present truth" to each generation of the church, encouraging and strengthening the faith of the remnant as they have seen the final acts in the drama of redemption drawing ever nearer.

But just as the false "scribes" in the days of Jesus failed to recognize the divine purpose in the first advent of Jesus, so, down the ages, false teachers in high places have all too often been equally heedless of "the present truth" of God's activity in history. And in our day, when His purposes are moving rapidly to their climax in the second advent of Jesus, many religious teachers are as incapable of discerning the "signs of the times" as were the scribes and Pharisees.

As in Christ's day those who most loudly proclaim their "apostolic succession" reveal, by their rejection of "present truth," that they comprehend neither the "new things" of God's activity nor the "old."

And so again God is compelled to set aside the unfaithful "scribes" who have betrayed their trust, and raise up others who will faithfully dispense "things new and old" to seeking souls.

The true "apostolic succession" in our day, as in Christ's, are not those who claim the authority of the so-called "historic church," but those who are proclaiming the "everlasting Gospel" in the light of the "present truth" for our time.

This chapter is based on Matthew 13:51, 52.

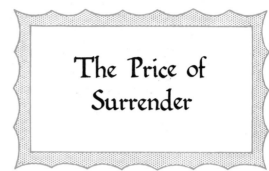

The Price of Surrender

THE parables of Jesus made a profound impression upon those who came to listen. Some immediately and unhesitatingly gave their hearts to Him and became His devoted followers. Others, typical of multitudes in our own day, would fain have followed Him, but for one reason or another they hesitated.

It was at the end of a long day of teaching, when most of the crowd had departed, that two of the hearers remained behind to talk personally with Him. How plausibly they put their problems to Jesus, and how penetratingly, yet kindly, He exposed their excuses.

Jesus' first interview was with a scribe who, like Nicodemus, recognized Jesus as a "teacher sent from God" and longed for power in his own life.

Bowing low before Jesus, he began eagerly, "Master, I will follow Thee whithersoever Thou goest." He seemed sincere enough and one might have expected Jesus to welcome so prominent a convert. But he did not, for He saw that in the man's first enthusiasm he had not realized what association with Jesus would mean to his position and prospects.

So, before accepting the scribe as one of His followers, Jesus frankly set before him the inevitable consequences of his decision. "The foxes have holes," He said, "and the birds of the air have nests; but the Son of man hath not where to lay His head."

How will you feel, He said in effect, if you are cast out of the synagogue as I was at Nazareth? Are you willing to accept the privations and hardship which are My lot? My disciples can expect no better treatment than is accorded to Me, and I am "despised and rejected of men; a Man of sorrows, and acquainted with grief."

The fact that the scribe's answer is not recorded suggests that he reacted like

---

As Jesus taught from city to city, many unhesitatingly gave their hearts to Him and became His devoted followers.
By CARL BLOCH

the rich young ruler who came to Jesus on another occasion and who could not bring himself to pay the price of surrender. "How hardly," Jesus remarked òf that young man, "shall they that have riches enter into the kingdom of God!" And how equally hard it is for those who have worldly position, influence, ambitions, and prospects to count them but loss that they may win Christ. Not many in His day were prepared to make the sacrifice that Paul, who sat at the feet of Gamaliel, made. And in our own day it is still true that "not many wise men after the flesh, not many mighty, not many noble, are called." They are not prepared to pay the price.

As soon as the scribe had left Jesus, the second would-be follower stepped up to Him. "Lord," he began, "suffer me first to go and bury my father."

On the face of it the request was reasonable. All his life this man had honoured his father and his mother according to the commandment, and now it seemed that he only wanted to pay his last respects to a parent who had just died.

The situation, however, was not quite so simple as that. When Jesus replied, "Follow Me; and let the dead bury their dead," He was not seeking to belittle or discourage filial affection. But, mourning, like every other religious observance among the Jews had become a very ceremonious and protracted affair. So much so that those who were studying to be teachers of the law were released from obligation to engage in it lest their studies should suffer. Surely then, training in the school of Jesus demanded no less priority.

But there may have been more in Jesus' reply even than this. It is not by any means certain that the man's father was already dead. Very possibly he was still in good health and would live for years. If this was so the man's reluctance to leave home was prompted by the fear that his father might die while he was away and that the estate would be divided up without his knowledge. What it really amounted to was that he was more interested in the earthly inheritance that might be coming to him than in his spiritual inheritance in Christ.

Going straight to the root of the man's hesitation, therefore, Jesus said in effect, "If you want to follow Me you must do so now and without a thought for anything else. Let those whose trust is in earthly possessions bury your father when his time comes, and dispute over their inheritance, but you cannot serve God and mammon."

On another occasion when Jesus was talking with would-be disciples a third condition was made by one of them, "Lord, I will follow Thee," he said; "but let me first go and bid them farewell which are at home at my house." Once again the request seemingly so genuine, was brushed peremptorily aside by Jesus. "No man, having put his hand to the plough, and looking back," He replied, "is fit .for the kingdom of God."

To have gone home simply for the purpose of saying good-bye to his parents would not have been condemned by Jesus as "looking back." What the young man really wanted to do was to go back and discuss the matter further with his parents. But Jesus knew that if he did this they would exert pressure to prevent him casting in his lot with Him.

Perhaps they were very possessive parents who could not bear to think of their son leaving home. Maybe he was needed to care for the family business. It is even possible that they regarded Jesus as just another zealot who would sooner or later get Himself and all who were associated with Him into trouble, and they did not want their son to land in prison.

Whatever it was, Jesus told the man plainly that he must make the decision himself, there and then, while God was impressing his heart. If he went home and allowed himself to "look back" at the security and regard which he was leaving behind he would hesitate and be lost.

Again we are not told what course the young man followed, but Jesus clearly indicated that the call of Christ must take precedence over even the most precious of earthly ties.

When Jesus calls men to Him He never conceals from them that surrender means sacrifice. Those who would follow Him must be prepared to "leave all." In one case "all" may mean position and prospects; in another, material security and possessions; in still another, friendships and family ties. The sacrifice is never easy, and more often than not it is what is most fondly cherished, but Jesus can permit no rival in the hearts of His children.

Nor does Jesus ask those whom He calls, to follow Him without counting the cost. He warns that only "through much tribulation" we may enter the kingdom of heaven, and that only those who "endure unto the end" will be saved.

He does, however, make two wonderful promises to His disciples. "I am with you alway, even unto the end of the world," He assures them and adds, "My grace is sufficient for thee." And those who have taken Him at His word know that those two promises far more than compensate for all the sacrifice that He may ask.

This chapter is based on Matthew 8:18-22; Luke 9:61, 62.

Storm on Galilee

IT had been a long day for Jesus. Since early morning He had been teaching the people and disputing with the Pharisees who were always around trying to make trouble. Even after the crowds had gone away several would-be disciples had remained to talk with Him. Jesus was tired and needed rest. But if He were to go back to Capernaum there would be none for Him. Visitors would throng the house early and late. So Jesus asked the disciples to get a boat ready to cross the seven-mile stretch of water to the other side of the lake.

Along almost the whole length of the eastern side, barren hills, riven by wild and precipitous gorges, descend steeply from the high tableland of Jaulan, then Gaulanitis, the tetrarchy of Philip, to the shore, so that there was no level space for any large towns. Except for one or two small villages where the wider valleys opened out as they reached the lake, the shores were bare of habitation. Here Jesus could hope to find a quiet retreat for rest and communion with His Father.

So weary was Jesus that as soon as the boat was under way He went to the stern and, lying down with His head on the padded leather helmsman's seat, He fell fast asleep. This human touch is surely recorded to remind us that Jesus was subject to all the frailties of human flesh. He knew what it was to feel utterly exhausted, and sleep was as sweet to Him as to any weary toiler.

When they were well out on the lake the starlit sky suddenly clouded over and a fierce storm broke upon them. Storms, of course, are by no means unusual on Galilee. Due to its peculiar situation at the bottom of a deep basin in the hills, it is very common, just after sundown, for cold air to rush down the funnel-like valleys onto the lake, turning the quiet waters into a seething cauldron. A modern traveller staying at a mission house on the lakeside tells of the sudden descent of such a storm which

---

Stretching out His hands toward the tumultuous sea, Jesus bade the angry waves, "Be still."

blew in the windows of his bedroom and scattered broken glass all over the bed.

These sudden storms on Galilee are always worst in the winter when the cold north winds blow down from the Lebanon Mountains, and this fateful night in the Gospel story must have been about the beginning of December.

Hardened sailors though Peter and his companions were, it was the worst storm they had ever encountered, and with their sails hauled down they were soon drifting at the mercy of wind and water. Huge waves dashed against the sides of the boat and toppled over into the helpless vessel.

Forgetting all about Jesus in their anxiety to save themselves, the disciples began frenziedly to bale out the water. But it was impossible to keep pace with the inrushing flood. The vessel sank lower and lower until it was almost awash.

Realizing now that their lives were in jeopardy, the disciples remembered Jesus who still lay sleeping peacefully amid the clash of the elements. Shaking Him, they shouted above the roar of the tempest, "Master, carest Thou not that we perish?"

What a question to ask Jesus! How it revealed the weakness of their faith. If they had trusted Him they would have known that no harm could come to them while Jesus was in the boat.

As Jesus opened His eyes, He looked first into the terror-stricken faces of the disciples and then at the mountainous waves. Calmly, and without haste or fear, He rose and, stretching out a hand toward the tumultuous sea, He said, "Peace be still."

In an instant the wind dropped, the advancing waves sank back, and the night became calm and still. The storm clouds rolled away and the stars shone again out of a clear sky.

Turning to the frightened disciples Jesus said simply, "Why are ye so fearful? How is it that ye have no faith?" For a moment no-one could utter a word. They were awestruck at the miracle. Then they began to whisper excitedly among themselves, "What manner of man is this! for He commandeth even the winds and water, and they obey Him." Did they, in the calm of the night recall the words of the Psalmist: "He maketh the storm a calm, so that the waves thereof are still. Then are they glad because they be quiet; so He bringeth them unto their desired haven"?

In Mark's account of the storm there is the significant sentence, "And there were also with Him other little ships." Evidently many who saw Jesus departing crowded into nearby boats, determined to follow Him. Some of them may have put back to the shore when they saw the storm clouds pouring down from the mountains. But others were quite close when the tempest broke. How amazed they must have been when the wind suddenly abated and the sea became calm. But when they looked across the water and saw the disciples on their knees around Jesus they understood, and to their lips came the same question which the disciples had voiced, "What manner of man is this?"

God allowed the storm to break that night on Galilee to provide one more evidence of the "manner of man" that Jesus was. Already in His first miracle at Cana He had exercised creative power in turning water into wine. Now, in the storm on Galilee,

He revealed His absolute power over the forces of nature. When He who spoke the waters into existence commanded them, "Thus far and no farther," they could not but obey. Creation recognized the voice of its Creator.

But why did Jesus wait until the situation was, humanly speaking, beyond hope before restraining the force of the tempest? Was it not to teach the disciples a lesson of absolute trust which they would need in the even fiercer storms of trial and difficulty that were to descend upon them in coming days?

God has never promised His children that their path will always be rosy, or that they will always sail in smooth seas. On the contrary, the Psalmist reminds us that "the afflictions of the righteous" will be "many."

Sometimes when Jesus allows us to come to dire extremity we may, in the weakness of our faith, feel that He has forgotten us. We may even cry, in our distress, "Carest Thou not that we perish?" But Jesus is never unmindful of the trials of His people. His ear is never deaf to their cry. Even when He seems to sleep He is watchful of His own. He is as near to us as He was to the disciples on the lake, and while He is at hand, no harm can come to us.

The storm may roar around us and we may be tempest-tossed, but we are safe with Him. He delays His help only to help us more, and when we have learned our lesson, deliverance comes as He speaks the wondrous words, "Peace, be still."

"Be not faithless, but believing," is what Jesus would have us learn from such experiences. "I believe; help Thou mine unbelief," should be our prayer.

The miracle of the calming of the storm has an added significance when it is realized that wind and stormy sea are used in the prophecies of Scripture to represent the strife of nations. In the last days, in fact, Jesus declared that there would be on earth "distress of nations, with perplexity; the sea and the waves roaring."

To human eyes it might seem that civilization must be overwhelmed by the storm that is even now blowing up from the earth's far ends, and as Jesus so vividly foretold, the hearts of many today are "failing them for fear, and for looking after those things which are coming on the earth." But amid the storms of the last days Jesus is still the security of His people. Their hearts are at rest amid the turmoil, for they know that when the tempest reaches its height He will once again rebuke the winds and the waves of strife and sin, and the storms of time will be stilled in the calm of His eternal kingdom of peace.

This chapter is based on Matthew 8:18, 23-27; Mark 4:35-41; Luke 8:22-25.

CHAPTER

FIFTY-SIX

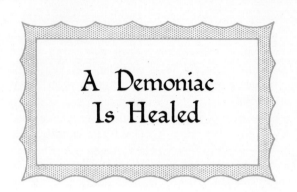

A Demoniac Is Healed

WHEN morning dawned upon the lake after the night of storm, Jesus and His disciples found themselves, according to Matthew's account, in the country of the Gergesenes, or Gerasenes. Mark and Luke call it the country of the Gadarenes. These variant readings, due to some scribal error in copying, pose a question as to just where it was that the boat landed.

The country of the Gadarenes lay at the extreme south end of the lake, the town of Gadara being perched upon a ridge overlooking the Yarmuk River some six miles from the shore.

It is conceivable, of course, that the storm could have driven the boat down the whole length of the lake, but against this the Gadara region provides none of the topographical features essential to the story which follows. At the southern end of the lake the mountains recede from the shore forming a considerable plain, so that there are no cliffs descending precipitously into the lake anywhere near Gadara. We are, therefore, compelled to look elsewhere for the scene of the drama.

Farther up the east side of the lake, and actually almost opposite Capernaum, is a ruin known today as Khirbet Kersa, in which may be recognized the ancient name of Gergesa or Gerasa and the still earlier Canaanite name of the tribe of Girgashites, who once lived there.

The ruins of Kersa, marked by the remains of a wall and some fragments of buildings, lie at the mouth of the wild Wady Semakh, or Valley of Fishes. The hills around are covered with a green and verdant sward ideal for grazing, and descend steeply, though not precipitously, toward the lake. Just south of the wady, however, there is a promontory which drops almost vertically to the beach, leaving only a narrow shelf between the cliff and the edge of the lake, which here is particularly deep. The nearby limestone cliffs are honeycombed with caves used in ancient times by the villagers as burial chambers for their dead.

Here is just the setting for which we are looking and we cannot but be con-

92

vinced that it was upon this rocky strand that the boat grounded and Jesus and His companions stepped ashore.

Jesus' intention in crossing the lake was to seek rest and time for meditation and prayer. The night had been anything but quiet and there was to be none for Him now. For, no sooner had they set foot upon the beach than an almost naked, shrieking scarecrow of a figure came racing down from one of the caves, followed by another as wild and unkempt as himself.

They were two dangerous madmen who, in days when there were no asylums for the mentally afflicted, had been driven out from the city and had taken refuge among the tombs by the lake. Remnants of the shackles, with which their neighbours had vainly tried to restrain them, still encircled their wrists and ankles, and their bodies were lacerated with wounds they had inflicted upon themselves in their paroxysms.

These poor sufferers were not just mental defectives. They were, like so many in Jesus' day, possessed souls in bondage to Satan. It seems as if the devil was seeking to do as much harm as he could to human minds in the vicinity of the Saviour in order to obstruct and frustrate His work.

Little wonder, therefore, that when the disciples saw them they retreated to their boats in terror. Only Jesus stood waiting, with infinite compassion in His face. as they advanced menacingly toward Him.

Anxiously the disciples watched, expecting the men to hurl themselves in a murderous frenzy upon their Master, when to their amazement the demoniacs suddenly fell at His feet and "worshipped Him."

They could not have known Jesus, for He had not been there before, and having been so long banished from human society, it is hardly likely that they had even heard of Him. It was the divine power of Jesus which subdued the devils and drew the poor men, quietened, to His feet.

But if the two captive souls did not know who Jesus was, the alarmed spirits which held them in bondage did, and it was their words which came from the madmen's lips.

"What have we to do with Thee, Jesus, Thou Son of God?" they cried. "Art Thou come hither to torment us before the time?" The evil spirits knew that Jesus was none other than the Son of God by whom they had been cast out of heaven with Satan. They knew, too, that they were destined inevitably for the abyss if they failed to defeat the purposes of God. No wonder that they were afraid and pleaded that they might not be tormented "before the time."

"What is thy name?" Jesus demanded of one of the spirits. "My name is Legion: for we are many," the spirit replied. On another occasion Jesus cast out seven devils from one poor creature, but here was a man in whom a legion of devils had found habitation.

When the devils realized that Jesus would no longer tolerate their presence they began to cast about for somewhere to go. Now it chanced that nearby a herd of some two thousand swine were feeding on the hillside in the care of swineherds from the town. We are not told to whom they belonged, but it seems likely that their owners were Jews, who, while not guilty of eating the flesh of swine themselves, made a good living breeding the animals and selling them to the Gentiles around. They must, indeed, have been very lax Jews for this practice was not only contrary to the whole spirit of the Mosaic law, but it was forbidden even by the rulers of the Jews, who could find a way round most inconvenient requirements of the law.

In these swine the devils saw the possibility of an alternative abode, so when Jesus commanded them to come out of their victims they "besought Him, saying, Send us into the swine, that we may enter into them."

Jesus knew what would happen if He acceded to their request, for if the spirits had turned normal human beings into raving maniacs they would do no less to these animals.

If the swine had belonged to Gentiles, Jesus would not have brought judgment upon them in their ignorance, but as their owners were greedy Jews who had sacrificed principle to gain, we can understand His readiness to teach them a needed lesson.

As soon as the devils entered into the swine, frenzy seized the herd and they stampeded violently down the slope. Reaching the steep bluff they were unable to stop and plunged headlong into the lake. The waters were threshed to foam as the panic-stricken creatures struggled to save themselves, but soon the tumult subsided and far and wide over the water hundreds of dead bodies floated away.

If it be thought unjust that the sins of their owners should fall upon these poor creatures it may be remembered that their end was swift and doubtless far more merciful than it would have been at the hands of the slaughterers.

When the swineherds, who had witnessed the catastrophe from the hillside above, realized what had happened, they rushed terror-stricken from the scene, fearful lest judgment should fall also upon them. Reaching the city they reported the disaster to their masters, stressing that it was not their negligence but the work of a holy man from across the lake.

Meantime, the two men from whom the evil spirits had gone out stood before Jesus transformed into normal human beings. Gratitude had displaced the blasphemous cursing on their lips and the hands that a few minutes before had been raised to strangle Jesus were uplifted in praise.

In this miracle Jesus once again vividly revealed the work He had come to do. These two men, long bound by Satan in body and mind and held "captive . . . at his will," had been released from their toils by the greater power of the Son of God. They were delivered not merely from devil possession, but from sin possession as well. They were literally "new men" in Christ Jesus and could well have said with the apostle Paul, "The life which I now live in the flesh I live by the faith of the Son of God, who loved me, and gave Himself for me."

One of the disciples ran to the boat and came back with some spare garments. Gratefully, the restored demoniacs covered their dirty and mutilated forms. Then, sitting down at the feet of Jesus, they listened enraptured as He talked with His disciples.

It was only about half a mile from the beach to the city, and so it was not long before the furious owners of the swine arrived, accompanied by other breeders who had herds out on the hills.

The story which the swineherds brought to them had been very confused and they did not really know what had happened, but when they saw the two notorious madmen, no longer naked and demented, but clothed and talking perfectly normally with the disciples, their fury was turned to awe and fear in the presence of the miracle.

When they had recovered somewhat, their anger returned and they determined that Jesus must be expelled forthwith before He wrought further judgments upon them. Like so many others in their day and ours, they preferred gain to godliness. They preferred to retain their sins rather than lose their swine, and to quiet their guilty consciences they were anxious to be rid of Jesus. So "they began to pray Him to depart out of their coasts."

Jesus did not remonstrate with them. Saddened by their callous selfishness He motioned to His disciples and started toward the boat. The Gergesenes did not want Him, but two poor souls in their midst had found salvation, and that had made His journey abundantly worth while. He would have come from heaven to earth for one soul.

The people of the country were relieved that Jesus was prepared to leave so promptly, but the restored demoniacs were loath to say good-bye to their Deliverer. Following Jesus to the boat, they besought Him to let them join the disciple band.

But Jesus had a work for them to do in their own country. They were known to everybody in the district. The villagers had seen them in their terrible maniacal paroxysms. They had driven them out to the lonely tombs by the lakeside. Now they would be living witnesses to the beneficent power of Jesus. Thus the wrath of men and of demons would redound to His praise.

So, gently relaxing the hold of one of the men upon Him, Jesus said, "Go home to thy friends, and tell them how great things the Lord hath done for thee."

When Jesus had climbed into the boat the disciples pushed it over the pebbles into the water and jumped in. As it gathered speed in the freshening wind they looked back to see the excited crowd gathered around the first missionaries to the Decapolis listening in awed wonder to their thrilling story.

Did Jesus lie down in the stern of the boat as it sped back toward Capernaum? He may well have done, for He had had little rest since He had left there the previous night. Yet though weary, Jesus was content, for He knew that His Father's hand had guided the boat across the stormy sea to open a door to the Gospel in that half-heathen land.

In the days that followed the healed demoniacs repeated their story not only in the nearby villages, but throughout the whole region of the Decapolis. So when Jesus returned nine or ten months later, He found a welcome awaiting Him and was able to minister to multitudes who came to Him.

This chapter is based on Mark 5:1-20; Matthew 8:28-9:1; Luke 8:26-39.

At Matthew's Feast

NEWS of the miraculous calming of the storm had been carried back to Capernaum by the "other little ships" that had followed Jesus out onto the lake, and His return was eagerly awaited. This was in striking contrast with the Gergesenes, whose one desire was to get Jesus out of their country as speedily as possible.

Among the crowd which quickly gathered round as soon as He stepped on shore there were, as always, many afflicted in body and mind who at once began to press their requests upon Him.

After healing and teaching for some time by the lakeside, Jesus was invited, with His disciples, to the house of Matthew-Levi, the tax-collector convert. Ever since his conversion, Matthew had wanted his old associates to meet the Man who had so influenced his life, in the hope that some of them might become His disciples, too. The Master's return to Capernaum provided a suitable opportunity and so Matthew quickly arranged a "great feast," calling in all his colleagues and inviting Jesus as the Guest of honour.

Matthew's friends were convinced that he must have taken leave of his senses when he gave up his post at the harbour toll booth to follow the new Teacher, but when they sat at table with Jesus and listened to His wise and kindly words many were drawn to Him just as Matthew had been. And though there is no record of the conversion of any of them on this occasion, we may be sure that the seed sown at Matthew's feast bore fruit in later days among these outcasts of society. The story is recorded also to remind us of our responsibility to witness to those who are closest to us.

The Pharisees and lawyers, who had been discomfited by Jesus at the house of Peter, were still in Capernaum watching for some new opportunity to accuse Him,

---

Jesus mixed with all classes of people, shunning none who needed His help.

and when they learned that He had gone to eat with "publicans and sinners" they hurried along to Matthew's house.

In the East, feasts are not private affairs such as those to which we are accustomed. Often they were held in an open courtyard and it was common for uninvited people to wander in to watch and even talk with the guests.

Remembering how Jesus had humiliated them at their previous meeting, the Pharisees and doctors did not attempt to reprove Him publicly. Instead, they sought to raise doubts in the minds of His disciples by suggesting that it was indecorous for Jesus, professing to be a spiritual leader, to be found in such company.

Jesus overheard the criticism and to expose their mock concern He said, "They that are whole need not a physician; but they that are sick." He would be a strange physician who never went anywhere near the sick in body, and where should a physician of the soul be found if not among those who were spiritually sick? They were supposed to be the leaders in Israel, yet they shunned those who were most in need of their help.

The Pharisees were actually sinners of far deeper dye than the publicans sitting around, but in their own eyes they were pre-eminently righteous, and so Jesus could do nothing to help them. He went instead to those who confessed themselves sinners to deliver them from their sins. There was irony in His tone when He added, "I came not to call the righteous, but sinners to repentance."

How many there are today in a like condition, satisfied with a "form of godliness," but farther removed from God than many an ignorant sinner. Such ones need to be reminded that now, as then, Jesus regards hypocrisy as the worst sin of all.

It was while Jesus was sitting with the publicans at Matthew's feast that there entered the chamber a ruler of the local synagogue named Jairus. He did not come to criticize like the Pharisees, but to seek the aid of Jesus in his dire need.

Prostrating himself before Jesus with his head touching the ground in oriental fashion, he begged Him to come at once to his house where his only child, a little girl twelve years old, lay "at the last breath."

This man knew Jesus well. As one of the college of elders who administered the Capernaum synagogue he had, on more than one occasion, invited Him to address the Sabbath congregation and he may have been one of the delegation who had waited upon Jesus on behalf of the centurion some little time before. Now in his distress he determined to ask help of Jesus for his own beloved child.

To his great relief Jesus rose from the feast, bade good-bye to the guests, and set off along the narrow street in the direction of Jairus' home.

In the throng which pressed around as He walked was a poor woman who had come a long way to seek Jesus, but now He was so close to her she was held back by embarrassment from presenting her need. For twelve long years she had suffered from a chronic and distressing hæmorrhage. She had consulted doctor after doctor, and had received all the treatments recommended in the Talmud for her complaint. But in spite of the nauseous drugs she had drunk and all the painful operations she had endured, her condition had grown steadily worse. With all her savings gone, she despaired of ever being healed until she heard of Jesus. Immediately she set out from her village to seek His aid.

She had hoped to speak with Jesus privately, but now, caught up in the crowd, she did not know what to do. Apart from a natural reticence to speak of her affliction in public, she realized that her condition rendered her ceremonially unclean and her presence in the crowd, if known, would certainly incur their hostility, and perhaps even the rebuke of Jesus. On the other hand, if she missed this opportunity, her last hope of being healed might be gone.

She was within arm's length of Jesus when an idea suddenly occurred to her. She had heard that others who had only touched Jesus had been healed by some power that went out of Him. Why shouldn't she do the same? "If I may but touch His clothes," she thought to herself, "I shall be whole," and no-one would be any the wiser.

Like all the teachers of that day, Jesus was wearing a close fitting rabbinical robe or kittuna of wool or linen reaching to His feet and fastened round the loins with a girdle. Over this an outer cloak, called a tallith, was loosely gathered around Him. At the four corners of this outer garment were the fringes prescribed by the Mosaic law, each consisting of three or four blue and white tassels several inches long, which were to remind the Israelites of the commandments of God.

One corner of the tallith which Jesus was wearing was flung over His shoulder and the tassels attached to it hung down behind His back. It was these which caught the eye of the poor woman. This was the most sacred thing upon the person of a rabbi. Surely it would be most potent in healing power.

Suiting action to her thought she stretched out her hand and touched the tassels. Instantly her hæmorrhage was staunched and she knew that she was healed.

Gratitude welled up in her heart for the miracle wrought in her, but she dared not make herself known now, for yet another fear came over her. It seemed almost as if she had stolen a blessing from Jesus.

She was just about to slip away through the crowd when Jesus turned and asked, "Who touched Me?" A chorus of denials came from those who were closest to Him, and Peter, always the spokesman, protested: "Master, the multitude throng Thee and press Thee, and sayest Thou, Who touched Me?" How could He complain of being touched in such a throng?

But Jesus did not mean the casual contacts of the crowd, and He said again, "Somebody hath touched Me: for I perceive that virtue is gone out of Me."

Seeing that her action could no longer be hid the woman fell to the ground before Jesus, confessing what she had done and how she had immediately been healed. Amazement spread over the faces of the multitude as they looked first at the prostrate woman and then at Jesus.

Trembling, she awaited His rebuke, but instead the gentle word fell upon her ear, "Daughter." Nowhere else in the whole Gospel record did Jesus ever call a sup-

OPPOSITE

partially restored syna-
gue of Capernaum. This
y be the very building in
which Jesus taught.

RIGHT

ornamental stone from the
Capernaum synagogue.

BELOW

k tombs outside the towns
villages were commonly
d in the days of Jesus for
the burial of the dead.

pliant by this tenderest of words. Then, as she gratefully lifted her eyes to His, Jesus went on, "Be of good comfort: thy faith hath made thee whole; go in peace."

How generous was the commendation of Jesus. Her faith really had been very imperfect, for she imagined that some magical property would be communicated from the garments of Jesus if she could but touch them. But, though imperfect, her faith was sincere and Jesus honoured it, at the same time correcting her limited understanding of the nature of His power.

Nor did His final words escape her, "Go in peace." She knew that she had not only received healing of body, but a peace in her heart such as she had never experienced before. Physical healing was, for Jesus, always an avenue to the soul, and the peace into which she entered that day remained with her all the days of her life.

In this miracle we once again recognize a parable of the hopelessness of sin and the wonder of the saving grace of God. Like this poor woman's disease, sin is chronic, defiling, and deadly. It is also beyond human aid. How many have gone hither and thither as she did trying one remedy after another to dispel the guilt of sin without avail. But though the sinner may fear in his uncleanness even to approach God, He never shrinks from the touch of faith. He who stretched out His hand to touch the leper and rewarded the touch of the afflicted woman will ever welcome the hand of faith outstretched for healing and pardon. This miracle has been recorded to assure us that however halting, however imperfect, our faith as we approach Him, if it is sincere, His "virtue" will flow out to heal and bless.

There is a story told on the authority of the early church father, Eusebius, that in order to preserve the memory of her healing this woman went back to her home in Cæsarea Philippi and had erected in front of it two bronze statues, one of herself

Stretching out her hands the afflicted woman touched the tassels on Christ's garment, and immediately she was healed.

By E. ARMITAGE

kneeling low before her Benefactor and the other of Jesus looking tenderly down upon her. Eusebius declares that he actually saw the statues there in his day.

Of course, we have no means of knowing whether this really was the home of the woman whom Jesus healed. More probably the statues were erected by some other sufferer who, inspired by the story in the gospels, sought and obtained healing from the same Source. If this be so it provides just one example of the thousands who have stretched out their hands in faith and have found help and healing as a result of this woman's testimony.

If God has done some great thing for you, therefore, you should tell it, too. Not that He needs your thanks, but your grateful testimony, like hers, may lead others to prove that His touch has still its ancient power.

This chapter is based on Mark 2:15-17; 5:21-34; Matthew 9:10-13, 18-22; Luke 5:29-32; 8:41-48.

The Raising of Jairus' Daughter

THE healing of the woman who had touched the fringe of His garment delayed Jesus for a while on His way to the home of Jairus, and the ruler was distraught with anxiety. When he saw his chief servant hurrying along the road toward them he knew instinctively the dread tidings that he brought. His beloved child was dead. When the servant reached them he confirmed the ruler's worst fears. "Why troublest thou the Master any further?" he said.

The message was half whispered to Jairus, but Jesus heard it, and, seeing the distress on the ruler's face, He said encouragingly, "Be not afraid, only believe."

Jairus hardly dared to hope that Jesus could do anything now, but somehow the quiet confidence of Jesus brought calm to his troubled heart as they hurried on to the house.

When they arrived, relatives and friends of the family were already extending their sympathy to the distracted mother, and professional mourners had been summoned to provide appropriate lamentation for the dead.

In those days the poorest family would have at least two flute players and one wailing woman. The ruler's family, being wealthy and influential, doubtless had many mourners, and the wails of the woman, the piping of the flutes, and the sound of beating upon bared breasts created a veritable pandemonium.

To Jesus the simulated sorrow of the hired mourners was repulsive, and as He entered the house He lifted His hand to command silence. When the tumult died down He asked the company, "Why make ye this ado, and weep? The damsel is not dead, but sleepeth."

A chorus of derision rose from the people in the room. Of course, the child was dead. They surely knew the difference between someone sleeping and a corpse!

Jesus leaned over the motionless form of the little girl and spoke to her. Immediately her eyes opened and she sat up. By CARL BLOCH

If they had not been so quick to scoff they would have realized that Jesus was not questioning that the child was physically dead, but was affirming that death is no more than a dreamless sleep if there is hope of an awakening. In the presence of resurrection power, death's hold is loosed and its sting is gone.

But Jesus did not permit them to stay and argue. With an authority they could not resist He waved them all from the room, leaving only Jairus and his wife and three of His disciples, Peter, James, and John.

Just when these three were selected by Jesus from the rest of the twelve to be His most intimate companions, we are not told, but this is the first recorded occasion that they were privileged to be the sole witnesses of some great moment in His ministry. Later, at His transfiguration, the three were again alone with Him, as they were also during His agony in the Garden of Gethsemane.

Motioning them to follow, Jesus went through into the inner room where the dead child lay upon her bed. Taking the little girl's hand tenderly in His, He leaned over her motionless form and said quietly, "Talitha, cumi," which meant, "Damsel, I say unto thee, arise."

Immediately her eyes opened. She sat up, looked around with a puzzled expression at the strangers in the room, and then jumped off the couch and ran to her parents, who clasped her in their arms in an ecstasy of joy. They could not believe that their daughter, over whom they had so recently wept in their distress, was alive and well again, and the record does not exaggerate when it says, "They were astonished with a great astonishment."

So far did they forget the child's immediate need in their excitement that it was Jesus who had to suggest that they should get something for her to eat.

As the ruler's wife ran to bring food and drink to set before the child, Jairus must surely have recalled the words of his servant on the way to the house, "Why troublest thou the Master any further?" Jesus is never "troubled" by anyone seeking His aid. Indeed we cannot seek Him too often. What troubles Him is to be treated with indifference by those who need Him most.

Nor can we ever ask too much of Him. However hopeless the situation, nothing is impossible with God, for it is His declared purpose to "save them to the uttermost that come unto God by Him."

Even death itself presents no final problem to Him who has the "keys" of death and the grave, and who is Himself "the Resurrection and the Life."

Sometimes Jesus delays to answer our agonized prayers until every human prop has gone to lead us to cast ourselves wholly upon Him. Then, in the extremity of our distress, we hear His assuring word, "Only believe," and we know that in His good time and way all will be well as it was with Jairus and his wife and their dear daughter.

This chapter is based on Mark 5:35-43; Matthew 9:23-26; Luke 8:49-56.

Every mother can enter into the feelings of Jairus and his wife when their beloved daughter was restored to them.

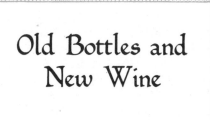

CHAPTER

FIFTY-NINE

Old Bottles and New Wine

F RUSTRATED in their attempts to humiliate Jesus publicly at Matthew's feast, the Pharisees and lawyers had angrily departed to think out a new line of attack. Soon they hit upon a subtle plan.

John the Baptist had been in prison for some time and his disciples were dispirited and in confusion. They could not understand why Jesus, whose coming John had announced, had done nothing to secure his release. They were perplexed also because He manifested none of the austerity of their master. Some were already aligning themselves with the Pharisees because of their seeming greater emphasis on spiritual discipline.

The Pharisees saw in this an opportunity of driving a wedge between John and Jesus. If they could get the disciples of John to denounce Him for failing to fulfil John's expectations, Jesus would quickly be discredited with the people who revered John as a great prophet. So, by playing one off against the other, they would get rid of both.

Perhaps it was on one of the weekly fast days in which Jesus and His disciples had taken no part, that the Pharisees persuaded some of John's followers to approach Jesus and chide Him for His neglect of this act of piety. The disciples of John fell into the trap and the Pharisees followed to witness what they hoped would be a show-down for Jesus.

"Why do we and the Pharisees fast oft," John's disciples began, "but Thy disciples fast not?"

Jesus might have replied by reproving them for yielding themselves as tools to the Pharisees. He could have pointed out that in the sanctuary year ordained by God there was only one fast, namely on the day of atonement, and that the osten-

---

Though opposed to one another in many things, the Pharisees and Sadducees were united in their enmity of Jesus.   By J. J. TISSOT

tatious humility of the Pharisees which had multiplied them to twice a week was not a sign of holiness, but a hypocritical pretence. But He did not enter into any argument. Very kindly He reminded the disciples of John of what their master had once said about the coming of the "Bridegroom."

John had spoken of himself as the "friend" of the Bridegroom and on seeing Jesus he "rejoiced greatly because of the Bridegroom's voice." Now, said Jesus, if the "friend" of the Bridegroom rejoiced at His coming, "can ye make the children of the bridechamber fast, while the Bridegroom is with them?"

There are many today who, like the disciples of John, mistake moroseness and asceticism for piety. Such a demeanour may actually be as hypocritical as the sad countenances and the ceremonious fasting of the Pharisees. If we are truly companions of the Bridegroom we must be happy, and the "joy of the Lord" will be reflected in radiant faces and buoyant spirits. People should be able to see that we have Jesus abiding, by His Holy Spirit, in our hearts.

Fasting and humiliation of soul do, of course, have a definite place in the life of the children of God. In the Scriptures they are often associated with seasons of special seeking after Him. Good King Jehoshaphat "feared, and set himself to seek the Lord, and proclaimed a fast throughout all Judah," in a time of serious danger. Daniel fasted and prayed in Babylon as he sought to know God's will for Israel. Ezra proclaimed a fast "to seek of Him a right way" for the returning captives. And in the days of Joel the people were exhorted to turn to the Lord in repentance "with fasting, and with weeping, and with mourning."

So also, declared Jesus, there would come times in the experience of His followers, when they would fast again. One day the Bridegroom would be forcibly taken from them and, in their terrible ordeal, they would fast and pray in agony of soul. But their hearts would be made happy again when He returned in His risen presence and bequeathed the Comforter to be with them for ever.

To us likewise there may come experiences from which we can emerge victorious only through fasting and agonizing prayer. But when deliverance comes, sorrow is turned to joy in His salvation. Joy and not mourning should be the dominant note in the life of the children of God.

Having corrected the erroneous thinking of the disciples of John on the relation of fasting to piety, Jesus turned to the larger issue raised by their drift back to the legalism of the Pharisees. The very fact that the disciples of John could speak of "we and the Pharisees" showed that they were under the same misapprehension about the teaching of Jesus as was Nicodemus at the beginning of Christ's ministry in Judea. Both imagined that a reform of Judaism, a new spirit in the old order, would satisfy God.

To Nicodemus, Jesus had revealed the radical difference between the Gospel and the teaching of the Pharisees when He said, "Ye must be born again." Now to the disciples of John He declared that the whole system of Jewish religion had become false and corrupt and would have to be replaced by a new spiritual order. The old order could not be restored by patching any more than one would put a "piece of a new garment upon an old." As new cloth would only make the rent in the old worse, so His message could not be woven into the worn-out cloak of the Jewish religion, because "the new agreeth not with the old."

Illustrating His point in another way Jesus said, "No man putteth new wine into old bottles; else the new wine will burst the bottles, and be spilled, and the bottles shall perish. But new wine must be put into new bottles; and both are preserved." The dry, brittle character of old wine skins fitly represented the loveless ceremonialism of the Pharisaic religion which could not but be shattered by the ferment of the Gospel. Only "new" men could contain the new wine of the Gospel, and only in reborn lives could its principles be exemplified.

Fundamental indeed was the truth Jesus was seeking to make plain. The white robe of Christ's righteousness is not given to patch the garments of self-righteousness, but to be worn as a new garment in place of our "filthy rags."

Continuing His illustration of the old wine and the new, Jesus pointed out that the necessary transition from the old to the new is never easy. "No man . . . having drunk old wine straightway desireth new: for he saith, The old is better."

Nicodemus found it a very hard thing to leave the ecclesiastical system in which he had risen to eminence, and it was not until long after his interview with Jesus that he made the decision. It was equally difficult for the disciples of John to realize the necessity of complete separation. But the disciples of Jesus, who had drunk deep of the new wine of the kingdom, knew which was best, as surely as did the guests at the wedding feast of Cana.

While Jesus, in His conversation with the disciples of John, was stressing particularly the incompatibility of Pharisaic Judaism and the Gospel, the truth He taught was to have a continuing application in the history of the church.

The early Christian centuries were marred by attempts to patch up Hellenistic philosophy and the Eastern mystery religions, producing "damnable heresies," of which the apostle Paul had to warn, and in the Middle Ages these perversions culminated in the great Roman apostasy. In the Reformation movement, therefore, God had to call upon His true children to "come out" and be "separate."

Down in the last days of earth's history, into which we are now come, the Scriptures reveal that Satan's final effort will be a gigantic attempt to shackle the spirits of men once again in the chains of the great apostasy. Evidence of this is already apparent, not only in the resurgence of Rome in the modern world, but in the increasing "Catholicizing" of the erstwhile Protestant churches. On every hand the claims of the "historic church" are being advanced, just as they were in the days of Jesus, to fetter the free movings of the Spirit of God, and many are being deceived. As Jesus counselled the disciples of John, we must resist the blandishments of these false ecclesiasticisms and be established in the "present truth" if we are to stand with Christ at His coming in glory.

This chapter is based on Mark 2:18-22; Matthew 9:14-17; Luke 5:33-39.

CHAPTER
SIXTY

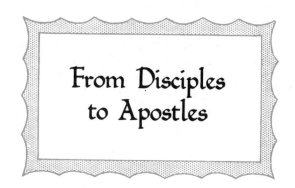

From Disciples to Apostles

I T was now some eight or ten months since Jesus had selected the twelve on the Mount of the Beatitudes in the spring of A.D. 29. Through the summer and autumn they had followed Him from place to place listening to His teaching and witnessing His miracles. Often He had also talked with them privately, explaining the deeper significance of the things He had spoken to the crowds.

In many ways the disciples had assisted Jesus in His ministry, controlling the crowds, bringing to Him special requests for help, and, as far as they were able, answering the questions of those who could not get near. Now He felt that the time had come for them to help Him in a more definite way.

As He travelled from city to city His heart was moved with compassion for the multitudes. Yet, limited by the physical frame which He had taken upon Himself, He could only stay a short time in any one place and then had to press on. More than once He had said to His disciples, "The harvest truly is plenteous, but the labourers are few; pray ye therefore the Lord of the harvest, that He will send forth labourers into His harvest." Now, they were to have a part in answering their prayers. The disciples were to become apostles and go out on their first evangelistic mission, revisiting as His representatives all the places in which He had preached and healed.

The limited objective of this first missionary assignment Jesus indicated when He commanded them, saying, "Go not into the way of the Gentiles, and into any city of the Samaritans enter ye not: but go rather to the lost sheep of the house of Israel."

The reason for this was that the period of Israel's probation, as outlined in Daniel's prophecy of the "seventy weeks" of years dating from the restoration of the

Jesus instructs His disciples in preparation for their first evangelistic mission to the cities of Galilee.

nation in the days of Ezra, had not yet expired, and until the Jewish nation had made its final decision for or against Jesus, the Gospel could not enter upon its universal mission.

So, for the present, the apostles were to avoid the Gentile cities like Tiberius and Sepphoris, and they were not even to cross the border into Samaria, but were to confine their ministry to the Jewish cities and the people of the covenant.

As Jesus had done, they were to declare, "The kingdom of heaven is at hand," and summon their hearers to repent and believe the Gospel. To give authority to their message Jesus bestowed upon them, for the first time, power "to heal the sick, cleanse the lepers, . . . cast out devils," and even "raise the dead."

For mutual support and companionship and to give their testimony added weight, He sent the disciples out "two by two." "Two are better than one," the wise old preacher declared centuries before, and the law of Moses likewise affirmed, "At the mouth of two witnesses, or at the mouth of three witnesses, shall the matter be established."

The association of the names of the disciples in the gospel lists gives us an inkling as to the pairs which were linked together. Vigorous Peter and his quieter brother Andrew made a good team, the former taking the lead, while the other was quite happy to give his support.

The brothers James and John doubtless went together, the organizing ability of James supplementing John's eloquence.

Philip is usually associated with Bartholomew, both faithful and solid if not "sons of thunder" like James and John.

Thomas probably paired up with Matthew and the other James with Jude or Thaddeus, leaving the zealot Simon to go with Judas Iscariot.

As one thinks of the ministry of Judas one cannot but wonder whether, in this first preaching tour, he gave any evidence of that fatal misunderstanding of Jesus which later made him turn traitor.

The mission of the first apostles to Galilee was literally a mission of faith, for Jesus told them not to make any special preparations for their itinerary, but go just as they were.

If a Jew were setting out on a long journey in those days he would certainly take a change of garments for Sabbaths and festivals, stout shoes to change into when the road became too rough for sandals, a staff to help him over the stony places and to ward off savage animals, and he would see that in the scrip or wallet in the fold of his girdle he had ample money to pay for lodgings on the way. He would take a sufficiency of silver tetradrachma or Roman denarii, perhaps even some Roman gold coins, as well as copper Herodian coins for small change.

The disciples were to take none of these things, no extra tunic, cloak, or shoes, nor even a staff. They were to take no bread in their satchels, "neither gold, nor silver" nor even the smallest "coppers" in their "purses." As labourers for God, Jesus promised that His providence would go with them and that all the hospitality they needed would be offered them on their way. For, He said, "the workman is worthy of his meat."

In accepting hospitality, Jesus counselled them not to seek out the homes where they would enjoy most comfort or luxury. Nor, like the Pharisees, were they to be over-punctilious or scrupulous about what was offered them. If hospitality was ready and sincere, however humble, it was to be accepted gratefully and a blessing of "peace" pronounced upon their hosts.

They were further advised not to move around like mendicants living on charity. Rather were they to make one hospitable home the centre of their ministry, "and there abide till ye go thence." Without doubt this was the origin of the "house churches," of which we frequently read in the early days of the church. These were the homes of converts who not only gratefully offered hospitality to the Gospel missionaries, but also opened them for the fellowship of believers and the preaching of the Word.

The apostles were to accept no rewards for their ministry save simple hospitality. Jesus never used His divine power for His own profit. He would not even make the stones of the wilderness into bread to satisfy His hunger. Nor were the apostles to seek gain for themselves by the exercise of their gifts. "Freely ye have received," said Jesus, "freely give." Salvation is not something to be sold or bought. It is a gift to be dispensed "without money and without price," to the poorest as readily as to the rich, and any who have violated this principle have incurred the severe displeasure of God. Gehazi was condemned to be a leper because he surreptitiously went after Naaman and took a gift which Elisha had very properly declined. Simon the sorcerer was promptly reproved by Peter for thinking that he could purchase the Gospel and then make a profit out of it. One of the worst sins of the papal church of the Middle Ages was that it enriched itself at the expense of those to whom it was established to minister.

At the same time, while the gift of salvation is free it should evoke in those who have partaken of its blessings a spirit of liberality toward the work of God. The support of His human instruments is not charity, but a grateful acknowledgment of spiritual blessings received.

So great was the apostles' task, and so short the time in which to do it, that a sense of urgency was to be ever with them. They were to be courteous to all, but they were not to indulge in the lengthy salutations and social visits so dear to Eastern peoples. These would absorb valuable time which should be devoted to their all-absorbing task.

What sort of reception were the disciples to expect as they went forth on their mission of preaching the Gospel of the kingdom? There would be those, declared Jesus, who would receive their message and help them on their way. Those who received them, He said, received Him and received God, and would be rewarded in the kingdom. "He that receiveth a prophet in the name of a prophet shall receive a prophet's reward: and he that receiveth a righteous man in the name of a righteous man shall receive a righteous man's reward." Even the slightest aid down to a "cup of cold water" to help a messenger of the Gospel would not be forgotten. "Verily I say unto you, he shall in no wise lose his reward."

But by no means all would receive the apostles or their message. As the ministry of Jesus stirred up fierce resentment, so the wider proclamation of the Gospel would arouse enmity in the unbelieving and unrepentant. Christ's messengers could expect no better treatment than their Master.

When they met with opposition in any place they were to take this as an indication that Providence was leading them elsewhere and, shaking the dust of the unbelievers from their sandals, they were to proceed on their way.

The significance of such an action would not be lost upon those against whom it was used. Among the Jews it was believed that the land in which a people lived partook of their character, whether good or evil. The soil of Palestine was holy for it was the dwelling place of the people of God, while the lands of the unbelieving Gentiles were regarded as unclean and unholy. Consequently, when Israelites returned from travelling in foreign lands they would shake the heathen dust from their sandals at the frontier that none of it might be carried over the border to contaminate the sacred soil of Israel. They would not even allow plants grown in heathen soil to be transplanted into the soil of Israel.

In the days of Jesus the practice had become a mockery, for the Jews had sunk into an apostasy which was no better than heathenism. Jesus therefore turned the symbolic act against themselves, foreshadowing the abandonment of the unbelieving Jews who rejected the message of salvation proclaimed by the apostles. "Verily I say unto you, It shall be more tolerable for the land of Sodom and Gomorrha in the day of judgment, than for that city," which for all its greater light knew not the time of its "visitation."

When Jesus had fully instructed the disciples, they went forth, in obedience to His command, "preaching the Gospel, and healing everywhere" throughout Galilee. "And they cast out many devils." Meanwhile, Jesus Himself did not remain inactive but "departed . . . to teach and to preach" in other cities.

How many places the apostles were able to visit during their first missionary tour we are not told, but it was certainly the most widespread proclamation of the Gospel of the kingdom up to this time and the name of Jesus was on every tongue.

How long the disciples were away on their itinerary the Bible also does not record, but it was probably something like two months. Then, at the appointed time, they all returned to the rendezvous Jesus had named near Capernaum to report. "And the apostles gathered themselves together unto Jesus, and told Him all things, both what they had done, and what they had taught." Everyone was jubilant, for the people had received them gladly and their first mission had been a wonderful success.

This chapter is based on Matthew 9:36-10:15, 40-42; 11:1; Mark 6:7-13, 30; Luke 9:1-6, 10.

Through Trial to Triumph

WHEN the disciples returned from their first evangelistic mission they doubtless imagined that this would be the pattern of their ministry until their Master was recognized as the Messiah and His kingdom was established. Only after Jesus had left them and ascended to heaven did they begin to realize the magnitude of the task upon which they had embarked and recall some other things He had said to them concerning the tribulations which the messengers of the Gospel would experience before the triumphal coming of the kingdom.

"Behold," Jesus warned, "I send you forth as sheep in the midst of wolves." The savage cruelty of ravening wolves aptly expressed the hatred of those who pursued Jesus to His death, and in the carrying out of their mission the apostles could expect no gentler treatment. Frustrated by the resurrection of Christ, Satan would intensify his assaults upon the church in order to prevent their carrying out the command, "Go ye into all the world, and preach the Gospel to every creature."

Yet, under constant attack, the messengers of the Gospel, like Jesus, were to pursue their task with the innocence of lambs and the gentleness of doves. While Jesus fearlessly rebuked iniquity and warned sinners of the inevitable consequences of rebellion against God, He spoke the truth always in love. With tender solicitude for the ignorant and erring He worked for the saving of the lost, and with His dying breath He prayed, "Father, forgive them; for they know not what they do." The same spirit was to characterize His messengers as they continued the work He had begun.

Though the disciples were to proclaim a Gospel of peace which would impart peace to the hearts of those who received it, it would also arouse variance and strife on the part of those who refused to hear it. "Think not," Jesus said, "that I am come to send peace on earth: I came not to send peace, but a sword." The Gospel would, in fact, be "sharper than any two-edged sword," dividing nations, communities, and even families where its message was accepted by some and refused by others.

117

"I am come," Jesus sadly declared, "to set a man at variance against his father, and the daughter against her mother, and the daughter-in-law against her mother-in-law. And a man's foes shall be they of his own household."

The challenge of the Gospel would compel men to choose between social and family ties and Jesus. And He added, "He that loveth father or mother more than Me is not worthy of Me: and he that loveth son or daughter more than Me is not worthy of Me."

Jesus' own family turned against Him and the messengers of the Gospel were likewise to have the terrible experience of seeing brother deliver brother "to death, and the father the child: and the children shall rise up against their parents and cause them to be put to death," because of the Gospel. How tragically this prophecy was fulfilled when pagan families betrayed Christian converts in ancient Rome and when "heretics" were denounced by their own kith and kin in the days of papal Rome.

Against the unremitting onslaughts of wicked spirits and evil men God's messengers might seem weak and helpless, but He would ever be their strength. He would give them the wisdom of serpents to counter the serpent's wiles. In the prosecution of their work they were not to invite persecution, though they were never to compromise their message in order to avoid it. Just as Joseph and Mary fled from Herod into Egypt and Jesus left Nazareth for Capernaum when His own townsmen turned against Him, the cause of the Gospel in time of persecution might often be served best by fleeing into another city where souls were waiting to respond to the call of God. If one door closed against them another would open somewhere else. Nevertheless, warned Jesus, if they were faithful to their task they would have to bear their cross as He bore His.

"Beware of men," He said, "for they will deliver you up to the councils, and they will scourge you in their synagogues" perhaps up to "forty stripes save one" as Paul endured on more than one occasion. "Ye shall be brought before governors and kings for My sake." "Ye shall be hated of all men for My name's sake."

But when they were delivered up, Jesus counselled them, they were not to worry unduly about how they would defend themselves. "Take no thought how or what ye shall speak: for it shall be given you in that same hour what ye shall speak. For it is not ye that speak, but the Spirit of your Father, which speaketh in you." Such testimony before the high ones of the earth, like that of Paul before Felix and Agrippa, would be a witness for the Gospel which otherwise they might never receive. And it would prove a "testimony against them" if they refused to hear.

There might come times when, in the purpose of God, the supreme witness of the church could be given only through martyrdom. Should this be, His people were not to fear "them which kill the body," for they "are not able to kill the soul." It would be their persecutors who would have cause to fear when they faced judgment at the hand of "Him which is able to destroy both soul and body in hell."

Those who rejected the message of salvation and despitefully dealt with those who bore it might seem for a time to go unpunished in their wickedness, but no evil deed against the servants of God or His cause would be forgotten. "For there is nothing covered, that shall not be revealed; and hid, that shall not be known."

Nor will God, who sees even the sparrow fall, forget one who suffers in Christ's cause. "Are not two sparrows sold for a farthing?" a sixteenth of a denarius, said Jesus, "and one of them shall not fall on the ground without your Father. But the very hairs of your head are all numbered. Fear ye not therefore, ye are of more value than many sparrows."

If His people faithfully confess Him before men, He promises that He will confess them before His Father in heaven.

If they lose their lives in His service, they will save them eternally in His kingdom.

So through "much tribulation," but ever instructed by God's Spirit and upheld by His sustaining arm, the church will bear its faithful witness until one day, "this Gospel of the kingdom" shall have been "preached in all the world for a witness unto all nations; and then shall the end come." And in that day, Jesus assures us, those who have endured "unto the end the same shall be saved."

Through the centuries which have elapsed since Jesus prepared His disciples for their glorious but perilous task, all that He predicted concerning the trials and triumphs of the Gospel has been accurately fulfilled.

We revere the heroes of faith who, even before the Scriptures were fully written, "had trial of cruel mockings and scourgings, yea, moreover of bonds and imprisonment: they were stoned, they were sawn asunder, were tempted, were slain with the sword: they wandered about in sheepskins and goatskins; being destitute, afflicted, tormented; (of whom the world was not worthy:) they wandered in deserts, and mountains, and in dens and caves of the earth."

We remember with gratitude the countless thousands since the days of the first apostles who sealed their testimony with their blood, and "loved not their lives unto the death."

And we rejoice that, despite the opposition of pagan emperors, papal hierarchs, darkest heathenism, and godless dictators, the Gospel of the kingdom has been extended to the uttermost parts of the earth.

Today the advance of the Gospel to the last outposts of mankind and the rising wrath of Satan as he realizes that he has "but a short time," combine to proclaim that the triumphant climax draws near, that the kingdom is "at hand," and the King is "at the door." God grant that when He comes He may find us working and waiting for Him.

This chapter is based on Matthew 10:16-39.

Art Thou He?

JOHN the Baptist had now been confined in the inner keep of the fortress of Machærus for more than six months. Day after day he looked out through the grating of his cell across the Dead Sea to the wilderness which for years had been his home, and to the meandering Jordan, in whose waters he had baptized, and wondered if he would ever be free again.

Because he secretly feared John, Herod had not harshly treated him, and his disciples were permitted frequent access to him. Whenever they came John eagerly inquired as to the activities of Jesus, but as time went on he became more and more perplexed at the course of His ministry. The corrupt priesthood still controlled the religious life of the nation. Vicious men like Herod continued to tyrannize over the people. The common people had expressed their desire to make Jesus king; they would have rallied to His standard if He had raised a holy crusade to establish His kingdom of righteousness, but He took no advantage of His popularity. Quietly, almost un-obtrusively, He went about healing and teaching men to love God and be obedient to His will. Moreover, Jesus had not lifted a finger to secure John's release from prison.

In his own mind and heart he was confident that Jesus was the Messiah. He had seen the Holy Spirit descend upon Jesus at His baptism, he had heard the voice of God from heaven pronouncing a blessing upon Him, and on the strength of this evidence he had proclaimed Him "the Lamb of God, that taketh away the sin of the world." But his disciples were constantly asking him whether Jesus was really the Christ or whether He was only another prophet and forerunner of Christ. John tried to encourage his disciples to believe, but he did not know how to reconcile Jesus' reticence, with the prophecies of the majesty and power of Messiah. At last he saw that there was only one way to convince them. He dispatched two of his disciples to ask Jesus plainly, "Art Thou He that should come, or do we look for another?"

Jesus sends the disciples of John the Baptist back to their imprisoned master with a message of comfort and assurance.   By C. DALSGAARD

It took them about three days to travel the seventy-five miles or so from Machærus to Galilee and they found Jesus just after He had sent the twelve out on their first mission. At once they put their question to Him.

Jesus might have replied to John's disciples as He did to the woman at Jacob's well, "I that speak unto thee am He." He might have plainly asserted His Messiahship as He later did to the man born blind, "Thou hast both seen Him, and it is He that talketh with thee." But he did not do this, because He intended to give them, and John, even more convincing evidence than that of His own words.

For a while, therefore, Jesus went on with His work of ministry, healing "many of their infirmities and plagues, and of evil spirits; and unto many that were blind He gave sight."

When all that came to Him had been helped, Jesus turned to John's disciples and said to them, "Go your way, and tell John what things ye have seen and heard; how that the blind see, the lame walk, the lepers are cleansed, the deaf hear, the dead are raised, to the poor the Gospel is preached."

Jesus knew that this description of His work would not be lost upon the imprisoned prophet John, nor on his disciples. They were well acquainted with the prophecies of Isaiah concerning the work of the Messiah, but, like so many other Jews of their day, they confused the prophecies of the earthly ministry of Jesus with those of the triumphant establishment of His kingdom. In His message Jesus quoted some of these Messianic prophecies in the thirty-fifth and sixty-first chapters of Isaiah to show them that the work He was now doing was the necessary preparatory work of the Messiah.

John, therefore, and his disciples could rest content that He was the One who was to come and that in due time He would fulfil all that had been said of Him. "Blessed," Jesus said to them, "is he, whosoever shall not be offended in Me."

We have no record of the conversation between John and his disciples on their return with the message of Jesus, but we may be sure that the evidence of fulfilling prophecy in the ministry of Jesus satisfied John. By it his confidence was confirmed that Jesus was the Messiah of God, and in patience he was prepared to tread with his Master the path of suffering which must precede triumph.

When the disciples of John had departed, Jesus turned to those who had listened to their conversation and gave a glowing testimony to the Baptist for his faithfulness in preparing the way of Messiah.

"What went ye out into the wilderness for to see?" Jesus asked. "A reed shaken with the wind?" Many a time as the people were fording the Jordan on their way to Jerusalem they had seen the tall papyrus reeds rising out of the shallow waters and crowned with tassels of wire-like hairs which swayed and rippled before the lightest breeze. Did John bear any resemblance to a trembling "reed"?

No, indeed. It was because he had fearlessly rebuked Herod's sin that he was now languishing in prison.

"What went ye out for to see?" Jesus continued. "A man clothed in soft raiment?" If John had been like the Sadducees and Herodians fawning upon the Herods, he might have been a court preacher "gorgeously apparelled," and living "delicately . . . in king's courts." But he had chosen a life of austerity and self-denial that he might do the work God had given him.

"What went ye out for to see? A prophet? Yea, I say unto you, and much more than a prophet. This is he, of whom it is written, Behold, I send My messenger before Thy face, which shall prepare Thy way before Thee. . . . Among those that are born of women, there is not a greater prophet than John the Baptist."

John was the last and greatest of the prophets who had testified to the first advent of Christ. To him was given the honour of announcing the Messiah to His generation. Yet, declared Jesus solemnly, great as was John, His forerunner, there was not one of His own true followers who was not greater than him. Not, of course, in the sense of surpassing him in dignity or in faithfulness, but rather in the new privileges of grace.

The typical services of the sanctuary and all the "prophets" had "prophesied until John" of the coming of the kingdom. Now had begun the mighty movement to which they looked forward, and souls were pressing into the kingdom with determination and holy violence!

Those who had ears to hear had responded to the call of the Baptist and they were now responding to the appeal of the Gospel. Yet how many who should have recognized the day of divine visitation were heedless both of John and Jesus.

John had come as an austere preacher of repentance "neither eating bread nor drinking wine" and they had accused him of being fanatical and possessed of "a devil."

Jesus had mixed freely with all classes, sharing their everyday experiences and proclaiming the liberty of the Gospel and they had accused Him of being self-indulgent and lax, "a gluttonous man, and a winebibber, a friend of publicans and sinners."

Like petulant children, Jesus said, they would not weep in sorrow for their sin nor rejoice in the coming of their salvation. But, He added, "wisdom is justified of her children." Many of the publicans and sinners, whom the Pharisees despised, had proved themselves to be true children of God by their acceptance of the Gospel, while the Pharisees and lawyers, for all their proud claims, had shown, by their opposition, that they were not the true children of Abraham or of God.

"I thank Thee, O Father, Lord of heaven and earth," Jesus declared of His day and ours, "because Thou hast hid these things from the [worldly] wise and prudent, and hast revealed them unto babes," in the estimation of the world. "Even so, Father: for so it seemed good in Thy sight."

Then in a timeless invitation, incomparable and inimitable in its beauty, He urged all who would escape from the frustrating struggle for self-righteousness into the peace and freedom of the Gospel, "Come unto Me, all ye that labour and are heavy laden, and I will give you rest. Take My yoke upon you, and learn of Me, for I am meek and lowly in heart and ye shall find rest unto your souls."

Can any resist such an appeal of love?

This chapter is based on Luke 7:18-35; Matthew 11:2-30.

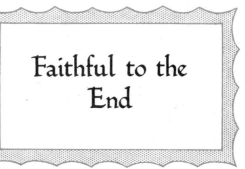

Faithful to the End

NOT long after John the Baptist received the reassuring message from Jesus the time of his martyrdom came. During the winter months Herod had accompanied the Roman legate Vitellius to Parthia to sign a treaty with the new Median king, Artabanes, and on his way back through Perea with his extensive suite, he decided to stop at Machærus where John was imprisoned and inspect the local administrators and military command. As his birthday was also at hand he decided to celebrate it there in Roman style with a sumptuous banquet.

Herodias and her daughter Salome were travelling with him or had met him; and on their arrival we can imagine Herod's wife looking up at the grim keep on the summit of the hill with hate in her heart, wishing she could find some means of putting an end to John's life while she was so near.

On an appointed day the nobles and high civil and military officers of Perea arrived for the banquet, and soon, across the still air of the palace courtyard, the shouts of drunken revelry reached the ears of John in his lonely cell. Did they convey to him an intimation of his approaching end?

According to the custom of the day, women were not invited to such feasts, so Herodias and Salome were not in the banqueting hall. But when the time came for the dancing girls to enter to perform their sensuous rhythms before the dissolute guests, Herodias conceived a crafty and evil plan. With no thought for the degradation of her lovely daughter, she sent Salome in to dance before her stepfather and the carousing nobles.

The abandoned company, their passions aroused by Salome's shameless performance,

---

All that Jesus predicted concerning the trials and triumphs of the Gospel has been accurately fulfilled as His messengers have borne their faithful witness to the world.

By A. A. DIXON

applauded vociferously and the intoxicated Herod was flattered by their approval. Calling Salome to him he rashly said to her: "Whatsoever thou shalt ask of me, I will give it thee, unto the half of my kingdom."

Excitedly Salome ran out of the hall to ask her mother what her request should be. This was the opportunity for which Herodias had been waiting. With clenched teeth she bade her daughter demand the head of John the Baptist.

Salome must have been deeply disappointed at missing the chance to ask for rich clothing and jewels, or even a castle of her own, but not daring to disobey her mother she returned to the hall and made known her horrible request: "I will that thou forthwith give me in a charger the head of John the Baptist."

An amazed hush swept over the drunken crowd. Licentious and brutal as they were, the demand of this beautiful girl shocked them.

Herod was distressed beyond measure, but he realized that he was trapped. If he refused Salome what she asked, he would be shamed in the eyes of all his nobles and he would certainly be upbraided by Herodias for sheltering John at the expense of her honour. There was nothing for it, therefore, but to bid one of his bodyguard go at once to the upper prison and behead John.

The executioner left the hall and in a few minutes returned with the head of the prophet on one of the golden dishes which a little while before had been piled high with the delicacies of the feast. Amid deathly silence he handed the gory dish to Salome, who took it straight to her mother.

The Bible does not record the loathsome scene in the anteroom of the great hall, but tradition has it that, taking a bodkin, Herodias thrust it through the tongue which had, in life, exposed her sin, and commanded that the headless body of the prophet be cast over the ramparts.

One of the palace guards, nauseated by the evil deed, must have sent word to the disciples of John to come quickly and take away the body before it was molested by carrion birds and wild beasts of the hills. With sad hearts, yet thankful that they could pay their last respects to their dead master, they went to the fortress, and after reverently burying John, they carried the tragic news to Jesus in Galilee.

If Herod thought that he would be able to forget the hideous crime and stifle his guilty conscience he was mistaken. The memory of the murder he had added to his adultery haunted him day and night, and when word reached him of the wonderful works which Jesus was doing in Galilee he was paralyzed by the fear that John had risen from the dead to take vengeance upon him. Though people were saying that Jesus was Elias or one of the other prophets come to life again, he refused to believe it. "It is John," he repeated again and again, "whom I beheaded: he is risen from the dead."

When, however, Jesus took no action against him he came to the conclusion that he must be wrong and dismissed the murdered prophet for ever from his mind. So blatant did he become in his sin that he even made sport of Jesus when He was sent to him by Pilate, and helped to drive Him to His death.

But retribution and ruin for Herod were not long delayed. Aretas, furious at Herod's abandonment of his daughter, declared war on him and reduced Machærus, his nearest fortress, to a shapeless ruin.

It was the policy of the Cæsars to keep the peace as far as possible with nations beyond the frontiers of the empire, and the reigning emperor, Caligula, vented his displeasure upon the defeated Herod by heaping favours upon his kinsman, Herod Agrippa I.

The envious Herodias urged her husband to visit Rome and get back into Cæsar's favour. Herod argued the danger of such a plan, but weak and vacillating as he had always been, he was once more overborne by his wilful wife. The visit proved fatal. Agrippa, suspecting the intentions of Antipas when he learned that he had gone to Rome, sent messengers to accuse him of treasonable plotting. Caligula believed the report and banished Herod and his wife in A.D. 39 to Lugdunum in Gaul, where both perished in misery and dishonour.

Salome married her uncle, Philip, tetrarch of Trachonitis and Gaulanitis, but she, too, came to a violent end. Falling through the ice on a frozen lake, it is said, she was drowned, her own head ironically being almost severed by the sharp ice before her body was recovered. So perished Herod and his infamous family for the murder of the Baptist.

John's end was indeed a tragic one and some might wonder why God did not intervene to prevent it. At any time after Lucifer's fall, God could have put a closure on the ravages of Satan against the faithful people of God, but He chose to allow Satan to do his worst in order fully to reveal the dire consequences of that first rebellion against heaven.

In His providence, He permitted all but one of the disciples of Jesus to die by the hand of their enemies as an example of faithfulness unto death to the multitudes of others, who, down the ages, have followed their Lord through tribulation to ultimate victory.

In the last days the Scriptures reveal that Satan will launch his most virulent onslaught upon the remnant people of God with the intention of completely obliterating them. But God's eye will be upon His people and at the time of His appointing, Christ will return to destroy the destroyer and deliver His own.

In that day the martyrs of the ages will come forth from their graves to see God's judgment upon their murderers. And with them John will be raised to witness the final triumph of the Christ whose first advent he heralded and in whose cause he was "faithful unto death."

This chapter is based on Mark 6:14-29; Matthew 14:1-12; Luke 9:7-9.

A Wonderful Meal

THE widespread witness of the apostles in the cities of Galilee had raised the popularity of Jesus to new heights, and His return to the neighbourhood of Capernaum brought still greater crowds to hear His teaching and seek His healing touch. Added to the multitudes from the cities and villages of Galilee were many pilgrims coming down the roads from the north on their way to the Passover, who broke their journey to see Jesus. In consequence, so great were the demands upon Him that neither He nor His disciples had "leisure so much as to eat."

Jesus never spared Himself when there was work to be done, but because He had taken upon Himself a physical frame common to men, the pressure of ministry told heavily on Him and both He and His disciples were in need of physical rest and refreshment, as well as the spiritual reinforcement of quiet communion with God.

There were other reasons, too, why Jesus wanted to leave the neighbourhood of Capernaum. Herod was now thoroughly alarmed by what he had heard concerning Jesus and there was every likelihood that he might seek to arrest Him as he had John. Jesus was not afraid of Herod and He knew that nothing could happen to Him until His work was done. But at this time He did not wish to further arouse his hostility or give him cause to think that He was fostering a rebellion.

Jesus could have departed from Galilee with the Passover crowds, but this would have been no rest for Him and it might have precipitated a crisis in Jerusalem.

So He decided to miss the Passover that year (A.D. 30) and seek, with His disciples, a quiet retreat across the Sea of Galilee in the territory of the tetrarch Philip. "Come ye yourselves apart into a desert place," He bade His companions, "and rest a while."

The last time they had crossed the lake they landed at Gergesa right opposite

---

Accepting the humble gift of a small boy's lunch, Jesus miraculously multiplied it to feed five thousand souls.   By J. F. CAMPBELL

Capernaum, but this time Jesus directed the disciples to turn the boat northward toward a "desert place" just east of the point where the Jordan entered the lake.

Here the slopes of the high plateau of Gaulanitis enclosed a little plain about two miles long and a mile wide, which today is called El Batiha. The nearest town in Jesus' day was Bethsaida Julias, some miles to the north, so called because the original obscure hamlet had recently been beautified by the tetrarch Philip, in honour of Julia, daughter of the Roman Emperor, Augustus.

While the plain was described as a "desert place" by reason of its comparative remoteness and sparse population, it was by no means barren or desolate. At this season of the year it was green with springing grass. It was indeed a delightful spot, far from the crowds which thronged the Great North Road down the lakeside, and a perfect retreat for Jesus and His disciples.

But the eager populace were not going to allow Jesus to escape so easily from them. Some had noted the direction taken by the boat and immediately began to follow it along the shore, crossing the Jordan by a ford a mile or so up the river. As a result, by the time the boat reached the beach a crowd was streaming across the plain as large as that which He had left behind.

As Jesus stood upon a little eminence looking at the approaching multitude, they appeared to Him like a flock of sheep wandering without a shepherd. Their spiritual needs should have been met by the priests, but they had been turned away unsatisfied.

Tired as He was, Jesus was moved with compassion at the sight of the people. Beckoning them to come near to Him He sat down and began to "teach them many things."

About three o'clock in the afternoon, as the sun began to sink toward the western hills, the disciples became concerned as to what the crowds would do in this remote place when night fell. It was a long way to Bethsaida and farther still to other cities, and if they set off right away it would be almost too late to buy food by the time they reached them.

So they approached Jesus and said to Him, "This is a desert place, and now the time is far passed: send them away, that they may go into the country round about, and into the villages, and buy themselves bread: for they have nothing to eat."

Of course, Jesus was just as aware as the disciples of the oncoming of the evening and He had already decided what He was going to do. Unlike the priests He had no intention of turning the people away empty. But to test the disciples' faith, He said to them, "They need not depart; give ye them to eat."

They almost laughed at the suggestion. They did not carry around enough food for such a multitude and even if there were any chance of buying it locally, Philip pointed out that the total amount they had in the common purse, about two hundred pence, equivalent in our money to seven or eight pounds, would not buy enough for each to have even "a little." Philip was not far out in his calculations, for a "penny" or a denarius, the commonest Roman silver coin, was a day's wage for a labourer and would buy food enough to feed probably five dependent members of his family. Two hundred denarius' worth of bread, therefore, would provide a meal for something like three thousand people. For nearly twice that number there certainly would be only "a little."

Jesus made no comment on Philip's quick calculation of their resources, but asked, "How many loaves have ye? go and see."

Several of the disciples went to make inquiries, and Andrew soon came back with the word that they had found one small boy whose food pouch contained five coarse barley cakes such as were eaten by the poorer peasants, barley being about a third of the price of wheat flour, and two small dried and salted fish about the size of sardines or pilchards, commonly used as a relish.

"What are they among so many?" asked practical Andrew in despair.

But Jesus took no more notice of Andrew's pessimism than He had done of Philip's. Instead He told the disciples to arrange the crowd in orderly rows, literally "furrows," of fifty or a hundred on the green turf, for convenience of serving. In their various coloured garments of blue and yellow and red they must have presented a lovely picture as they spread out over the plain.

It was when this had been done that the disciples realized that there were no fewer than "five thousand" men in the crowd beside the "women and children" who, according to oriental usage, were not actually counted.

The little peasant boy could scarcely conceal his excitement when he saw the disciples give his meagre lunch to Jesus. Jesus could have produced a meal for the multitude out of nothing just as easily, of course, but by accepting the humble offering He wanted to show how He values the gifts of His children and how, with His added blessing, they can be multiplied to His glory.

Gathering the disciples around Him, Jesus raised His hands in blessing 'upon the loaves and fishes. Maybe He used the form of blessing commonly spoken in Jewish households in those days: "Blessed art Thou, Jehovah our God, King of the world, that causest bread to come forth out of the earth." When we say grace before meals we acknowledge that all our food, though produced in part by human effort, is a gift from God's hand.

When He had prayed, Jesus began to break the loaves and divide the fishes, and as He did so they were multiplied in His hands so that basket after basket was filled as the amazed disciples brought them to Him. When it states that Jesus "gave" the food to the disciples to distribute, it means literally that He "kept on giving" to them, suggesting an unending multiplication of the pieces as the cakes were broken in His hands.

It should not escape our notice as we read the story of this wonderful miracle that while Jesus miraculously multiplied the loaves and the fishes He did not change their nature. He did not turn the poor barley loaves into fine wheaten bread. Nor did He cause the little fishes to turn into some more delicately tasting fish. God does not promise luxury as a consequence of following Him. He never panders to self-indulgence, which more often leads men away from Him. But He does assure us that

OPPOSITE

Palestine shepherd with some of his flock.

ABOVE

wing water for the flock at a wayside well.

RIGHT

pherds lead their sheep ng a road in Palestine.

in His service our "bread" and "water," that is, the simple requirements of life, will never be lacking. And on this occasion the humble fare which Jesus provided became a princely repast better far than the luxurious but profane table in Herod's palace.

Along the ranks of the seated multitudes the disciples moved with the laden baskets, coming back as soon as they were empty for more from the never-ending supply until everyone had received "as much as they would."

In this miracle Jesus once again revealed His divine power. At Cana He had turned water into wine. Here He miraculously multiplied a little boy's lunch to feed a multitude. In a moment of time He carried out the creative work which, through the slower operation of nature's laws, results in the regular harvests of field and orchard. The latter, no less than the former, are the work of a miracle-working God and should evoke the gratitude and worship of man.

Materialistic science is all too prone to explain the operations of nature as the result of "natural law," forgetting that there can be no law without a Law-giver and no creation without a Creator.

The miracles of Christ should remind us of the ceaseless miracles of nature by which God opens His hand and satisfies "the desire of every living thing."

In the feeding of the five thousand, Jesus revealed His constant care for the physical as well as the spiritual needs of His people, and in so doing He emphasized the church's continuing responsibility to deal their "bread to the hungry," to "satisfy the afflicted soul," to "cover" the "naked," and to care for the "poor that are cast out," as well as preach to them the Gospel of their souls' salvation.

To the church today, Jesus says, as He looks upon suffering humanity, "Give ye them to eat," and in the judgment He will have the special commendation for many, "I was an hungered, and ye gave Me meat."

At the same time Jesus wanted those who received material bread at His hands to realize that He had come not merely to relieve their physical needs, but to bring to them the true spiritual Bread.

A little later He had occasion to reprove some for having missed the real purpose of His mission. "Labour not," He urged them, "for the meat which perisheth, but for that meat," the Bread of life, "which endureth unto everlasting life."

At last the wilderness meal was ended, but Jesus had not yet finished His spiritual object lesson. Before the people rose, He commanded the disciples to go again among the crowd and gather up the fragments which remained, not the bits which had fallen on the ground, but the pieces still remaining in the baskets scattered among the people. And when they put them all together they found that they had twelve baskets full, far more than the five loaves and two fishes with which Jesus had started.

If Jesus had wished, He could have multiplied the loaves and fishes to just the quantity needed to feed the multitude without any being left over. There must, therefore, be a reason why He chose to provide more than enough to meet their needs. And surely it was to show that His blessings, temporal and spiritual, are bestowed, not grudgingly but with a bounteous hand, "pressed down, and shaken together, and running over."

At the same time He was careful to have all that was not eaten at the time gathered up for future use. For while the miracles of Jesus are to encourage us to trust Him in time of need, they are not to make us careless and improvident in our use of His bounty.

Then beyond all the precious lessons which the miracle of the loaves and fishes has for us in this life, this wonderful meal gives us assurance of the more abounding heavenly provision which Jesus is even now making for His people. It reminds us that one day soon, all who have followed Him through the "wilderness" of this world will be invited to sit down with Him to partake of the inexhaustible provisions of His kingdom where none will hunger nor thirst any more.

This chapter is based on John 6:1-14; Mark 6:30-44; Matthew 14:13-21; Luke 9:10-17.

Basket after basket was filled as the amazed disciples brought them to Jesus.
By L. M ROTH

CHAPTER SIXTY-FIVE

Saved From the Storm

THE miracle of the loaves and fishes, which climaxed the ministry of Jesus on that wonderful day in the wilderness, convinced the multitude that He must be the long-awaited Messiah. Many had heard His conversation with the disciples of John when they had plainly asked, "Art Thou He that should come?" and now they began excitedly to say among themselves, "This is of a truth that Prophet that should come into the world," for none but He could do such wonders.

Then, with one accord, they surged forward to acclaim Him their Deliverer and King.

The disciples were as excited as the people by the dramatic turn of events. To them it seemed that the kingdom Jesus had talked about so often was about to be realized and they waited expectantly to see what He would do.

Great was their disappointment when He turned to them and bade them return quickly to the boat and prepare to leave, while He sent the people away.

At first they protested vigorously. They could not understand why He did not take advantage of the enthusiasm of the multitude. They felt that He was throwing away a golden opportunity of securing their allegiance.

But Jesus "constrained" them and finally, much against their will, and still murmuring among themselves, they turned toward the beach.

The people were equally impatient as Jesus waved them back and urged them to disperse. The leaders even sought to take Him by force and proclaim Him their King. But firmly Jesus bade them leave, and gradually the disappointed multitude melted away in the gathering dusk.

When all had gone the disciples expected Jesus to come down and join them,

As Peter felt himself beginning to sink, he cried out in terror. In a moment he was safe in the arms of Jesus.

By B. PLOCKHORST

but instead He turned toward the hills and they knew that He had gone away alone to pray.

Jesus had need to commune with His Father, for He had come to a turning-point in His earthly life. He knew that the popular conception of the Messiah was that of a mighty Deliverer who would liberate His people from their long bondage, and that the great majority had followed Him in the belief that their hope was now to be realized. He had tried to show them that His mission was to save them from their sins rather than to free them from the Roman yoke, but so obsessed were they with the hope of national deliverance that they persisted in misunderstanding Him. Even the disciples failed to recognize that He must be the suffering Servant before He could become the mighty King.

In the presence of this great multitude, Jesus had deliberately refused to assume the leadership in a crusade for national freedom and He had seen their enthusiasm vanish in disillusion. He knew that before long disillusion would turn to a hatred which would hound Him to His death.

As darkness descended upon the towering hills, Jesus glimpsed the shadows which had already begun to fall upon His earthly pathway. And alone with His Father He prayed for His disciples in their blindness and for strength to tread the tragic path which stretched before Him to the cross.

The disciples waited until dark for Jesus to return, but He did not come. So they decided to leave, believing that Jesus would walk round the head of the lake and meet them in Capernaum. They were still bitter about the lost opportunity and intended to raise the matter again when He rejoined them.

No sooner had they set sail than the fresh wind turned to a wild gale, which was soon lashing the waters into foaming waves. Quickly they hauled the canvas down to save the boat from capsizing and began laboriously to row against the battering waves.

They had only about six miles to go across the north end of the lake, but, by the "fourth watch," or around three o'clock in the morning, they were no more than half-way over and worn out by the struggle against wind and wave. Suddenly out of the darkness a glistening white form appeared, walking past them upon the water.

Thinking that it was an angel of destruction, betokening disaster and death, they cried out in terror. Great was their surprise and relief when a clear and familiar voice sounded above the din of the storm, "Be of good cheer: it is I; be not afraid." Then they saw that it was none other than Jesus.

All through that terrible night they had thought themselves alone on the storm-tossed lake. The memory of the miracle in the wilderness had faded from their minds and Jesus seemed to have passed out of their lives. But from His place of prayer He had been watching their painful voyage through the night. He had allowed the storm to overtake them because of their impatience and unbelief, and He had waited until the last watch of the night, when they were at the end of their resources, to show them how helpless they were without Him. When, in agony of soul, they forgot their unholy ambitions and cried for help, He came to their aid and their hearts welled up in humble gratitude and love.

As usual Peter was the first to express himself, and, rushing to the side of the boat nearest to Jesus, he asked that he might come to Him on the water.

"Come," responded Jesus, and the impetuous disciple jumped over the side of the boat and stood upon the water.

Confidently he took a few steps forward, careless of the wind which tossed his garments, and the driving spray. Then, as a great wave curled up over his head, momentarily obscuring the form of Jesus, his faith failed him and he felt himself beginning to sink.

"Lord, save me," he cried in terror. In a moment Jesus was close to him and Peter was safe in His arms. "O thou of little faith, wherefore didst thou doubt?" Jesus said in gentle reproof as He led the trembling disciple across the water to the ship. When they had climbed in, the storm abated as quickly as it had arisen and the disciples, "amazed in themselves beyond measure," continued their journey through smooth water to the other side.

How typical of our own lives was the experience of the disciples on that wild night on Galilee. When darkness falls and the storms break upon us we may feel that we are forgotten and alone. But all the time Jesus is watching and waiting. Though we may not see Him, His eye is ever upon us, and always we are within reach of His power and love.

He may wait until the last watch of the night to teach us some needed lesson, but as soon as we have learned it, deliverance comes and the joy of His presence and benediction is ours again.

There is warning for us, too, in Peter's alarming experience. It is in moments of spiritual elevation, when God has done some wonderful thing for us, that we are most prone to self-exaltation and presumption if we but for a moment take our eyes off Him to whom we owe our deliverance. Peter needed to learn the lesson of distrust of self and constant dependence upon Jesus, and he had to pass through even deeper waters yet before he finally learned it.

Only as we continue to "look to Jesus," and depend wholly upon Him shall we be sustained and upheld amid the storms of life, until we are safely gathered into His arms in His everlasting kingdom.

This chapter is based on Matthew 14:22-36; John 6:15-24; Mark 6:45-56.

The Bread of Life

IT was so late, when Jesus dismissed the multitude in the wilderness, that many did not attempt to go home, but slept that night under the stars. The next morning they returned to the scene of the miracle in the hope of finding Jesus and persuading Him to reconsider their offer to make Him king. Much to their surprise He was nowhere to be found. They knew that the only boat on the beach the night before was that belonging to the disciples and they had seen it leave without Jesus. So in groups they scattered over the plain to look for Him, but in vain.

Just as they were abandoning the search, a number of boats from the southern end of the lake arrived. Their occupants had heard that a multitude had followed Jesus into the wilderness and they doubtless wanted to see Him too. On learning that He had gone they took as many of the people as they could with them back across the lake.

On landing they inquired after Jesus and could scarcely believe their ears when they were told that He was in the city teaching and ministering to the afflicted. It never occurred to them, of course, that He could have walked across the lake and caught up with the disciples' boat in the storm!

By the time they reached Jesus He had gone into the local synagogue, for it was one of the weekdays when it was open for services. At once they asked Him, "Rabbi, when camest Thou hither?"

Jesus did not satisfy their curiosity, but immediately reverted to the matter which was uppermost in their minds when they had parted the previous evening.

"Verily, verily, ..." Jesus said, "ye seek Me, not because ye saw the miracles, but because ye did eat of the loaves, and were filled." Their only interest in Him was in the material benefits which they believed He had power to provide. If He had

---

Back again in Capernaum after the feeding of the five thousand, Jesus went into the synagogue to teach.   By J. J. TISSOT

fed one multitude in the wilderness, He might work similar miracles elsewhere, and they wanted to be around to have their share again. But they had no desire for the Bread of life with which He offered to satisfy their spiritual hunger, or for the Water of life to quench their spiritual thirst.

They had, in fact, completely misunderstood His mission. They were thinking purely in terms of material advantage. Jesus was thinking of their souls. Their concern was for liberation from the Roman bondage. He had come to set them free from the bondage of sin. Once again, therefore, He said to them, "Labour not for the meat which perisheth, but for that meat which endureth unto everlasting life."

The Jews were annoyed when He suggested that their motives for following Him were material and unspiritual, and they hastened to defend themselves by asserting that they were only too willing to do anything they could to secure God's favour. "What shall we do," they demanded, "that we might work the works of God?"

Quietly Jesus replied, "This is the work of God, that ye believe on Him whom He hath sent."

How difficult it was for these proud and self-satisfied Jews to learn the lesson of faith. If He had called upon them to perform some arduous round of religious duties, they would have been quick to do His bidding. If He had called upon them to rally to His standard, they would have been prepared to die for His cause. But because He simply asked them to believe, they were disappointed. They were prepared to labour long and hard to earn salvation. It hurt their pride to have to accept it as a gift. Yet the work of faith was the greatest work which they could perform.

How common is that attitude in our day. So many are prepared to do all manner of works—alms, penances, religious acts of all kinds—in the belief that they are thereby meriting the commendation of God, but their pride is hurt when they are told that they can do nothing to gain salvation except believe on "the Lamb of God, which taketh away the sin of the world."

The truth is that many today, as in Israel of old, are too proud to be saved. It was pride which first separated man from his Creator, and a "broken and a contrite heart" is the first requirement for a reconciliation.

Embarrassed by the exposure of their lack of spirituality and pride, the Jews sought to cover up their confusion by questioning the grounds on which Jesus claimed their loyalty. "What sign showest Thou then, that we may see, and believe Thee? what dost Thou work?"

The previous afternoon they were prepared to acclaim Jesus as their King on the strength of the miracle of the loaves and fishes. Now they sought to depreciate it as insufficient to establish His claims. True, He had provided five thousand people with a meal of barley loaves and fishes in the wilderness, but Moses gave Israel "bread from heaven" for forty years in the desert of Sinai. To prove that He was greater than Moses, Jesus would have to do a greater work than Moses.

If He had wished, Jesus could easily have given the Jews some physical "sign" to show them beyond dispute that He was greater than Moses, but He had not come to subjugate men's minds. Rather had He come to win their hearts. So patiently Jesus sought to bring them to the realization of their spiritual need. God may have given them "bread from heaven" in the form of manna to meet their physical needs, but, He said, "My Father" now "giveth you the true Bread from heaven." This true Bread "is He which cometh down from heaven, and giveth life unto the world."

The manna which God provided by the hand of Moses supplied only their physical needs. After partaking of it they soon hungered again. Though it sustained their life for a time, they died in the wilderness. But in Jesus the Father was offering them the "true Bread from heaven" which conferred enduring "life."

Still thinking in material terms of some specially efficacious "manna" from heaven, the people quickly demanded, like the woman of Samaria: "Lord, evermore give us this bread." This would indeed give them the evidence they asked. If He would do that He could be sure of their allegiance.

When Jesus saw that they were determined to misconstrue His every word He said to them very plainly, "I am the Bread of life: he that cometh to Me shall never hunger; and he that believeth on Me shall never thirst."

The Jews were quite familiar with the idea of "eating" spiritual doctrine and "drinking" instruction. Jeremiah, among biblical writers, had said of God's Word: "Thy words were found, and I did eat them," and one of the lessons of the manna in the wilderness, as Moses pointed out, was that "man doth not live by bread only, but by every word that proceedeth out of the mouth of the Lord." But Jesus spoke not merely of "eating" His words or His teaching, but of eating Himself. Thus He showed plainly that He was not just a "teacher come from God," to impart the word of salvation. He was, in fact, the "living" Word. The life of God was manifest in the incarnate Christ, and if they would have life they must partake of His very being.

"I am the living Bread which came down from heaven," He said again: "If any man eat of this Bread, he shall live for ever: and the Bread that I will give is My flesh, which I will give for the life of the world."

Scoffingly the Jews asked of one another, "How can this Man give us His flesh to eat?"

Quickly Jesus retorted, "Verily, verily, I say unto you, ... whoso eateth My flesh and drinketh My blood, hath eternal life; and I will raise him up at the last day. For My flesh is meat indeed, and My blood is drink indeed.

"He that eateth My flesh, and drinketh My blood, dwelleth in Me, and I in him. . . . Except ye eat the flesh of the Son of man, and drink His blood, ye have no life in you."

In this reference to His flesh and His blood Jesus revealed for the first time the ultimate sacrifice of Calvary through which He would revivify dying humanity. His flesh and His blood are life to those who claim the merits of His sacrifice. Through them the dying sinner partakes of the divine nature and is revitalized by the divine life of the Son of God. Then he is able to say with Paul, "I live; yet not I, but Christ liveth in me."

Jesus could not have spoken more plainly. The Jews had been blind to their real need. The bread they were looking to God for was material prosperity; the life for which they yearned was renewed natural life. What they needed, and what Jesus came down from heaven to bring, was spiritual regeneration which would confer everlasting life.

As Jesus explained His mission He read disappointment and hostility in the faces of His hearers, and solemnly He pointed out to them the implications of their unbelief.

"All that the Father giveth Me shall come to Me," He said: "and him that cometh to Me I will in no wise cast out. . . . This is the Father's will which hath sent Me, that of all which He hath given Me I should lose nothing."

They might try to justify themselves and dispute His authority, but the Father had sent Him down from heaven to seek out His true children. These would believe on Him and follow Him. Not one would fail to respond and not one of God's true children would He reject. "Ye also have seen Me, and believe not." This showed that they had no part with Him or with His Father.

The Jews saw clearly what Jesus meant and immediately began to protest angrily among themselves. What right, they cried, had this Man to claim that He had come from heaven from the Father, and that only those who joined themselves to Him were God's children? "Is not this Jesus, the Son of Joseph, whose father and mother we know," poor peasants of Nazareth? "How is it then that He saith, I came down from heaven?"

Jesus could have revealed to them the mystery of the Incarnation, how that He had "emptied Himself" of His glory in order to come close to sinful men. But He did not do so because the people were determined not to believe in Him. Instead He repeated His indictment of their unbelief. "No man," He said, "can come to Me, except the Father which hath sent Me draw him." And "every man . . . that hath heard, and hath learned of the Father, cometh unto Me." If they were truly taught of God they would come to Him. But they did not hunger and thirst after righteousness, therefore they did not come that they might receive the Word of life.

As He spoke, His penetrating eyes scanned the crowd, compelling decision for or against Him. The sad record continues, "From that time many of His disciples went back, and walked no more with Him." By this they revealed their true character, their carnal desires, their selfish motives. They left Him because, in their tragic blindness, they failed to realize what they most needed.

And that is also the tragedy of the world today. If the church were to plunge into politics, concern itself with economic planning, and preach social reform, it would be popular; but when it proclaims the everlasting Gospel of spiritual regeneration and foretells the passing of the kingdoms of this world to make room for the kingdom of God, all too many designate it as "other-worldly" or contemptuously refer to its teachings as "pie in the sky," and turn impatiently away.

But it is nevertheless still true that the supreme need of the world is not deliverance from its oppressions and tyrannies and the alleviation of its physical hardships and miseries, though these have their definite place in the divine programme, but the spiritual regeneration of mankind.

The Jews thought that the message of Jesus was not relevant to their situation, and the great majority of people today accuse the church of irrelevance. The teaching of Jesus in His day was so "hard" to receive that few would "hear" it. And it is the same today. Yet only spiritual regeneration can save the individual. It only can save the world.

As Jesus sadly watched the crowd melt away He turned to His closest disciples who were anxiously whispering among themselves. "Will ye also go away?" He asked. He did not put this question to them because He doubted their loyalty, except for Judas. He knew what their answer would be and He wanted them to bear their testimony to strengthen those who were still wavering.

As usual, Peter assumed the rôle of spokesman. "Lord, to whom shall we go?" he asked. "Thou hast the words of eternal life. And we believe and are sure that Thou art that Christ, the Son of the living God." Peter and his companions knew from experience the joy and peace that had come into their lives since they had followed Jesus, and nothing could ever shake their confidence that He was indeed the "Christ."

"Have not I chosen you twelve?" said Jesus. But, He added sadly, as He looked around the little group, "One of you is My accuser."

Solemn must have been the faces of the disciples as they gazed at one another seeking to discover who would prove disloyal to the Master.

At this time Judas himself had no thought in his mind of betraying Jesus, but he had been foremost in criticizing Jesus for not accepting the acclamation of the multitude at Bethsaida, and he was becoming increasingly disturbed by His refusal to rally the people in a crusade for freedom and independence.

The words of Jesus could have arrested his disaffection had he been willing to listen. But he persuaded himself that his criticisms were in the best interests of their cause. So the seeds of disloyalty continued to grow until he made the fatal decision to betray Jesus into the hands of His enemies.

The tragedy of those who, after following Jesus for a time, turned back and "walked no more with Him," and the final and even more terrible defection of Judas, underlines the solemn warning that "we are made partakers of Christ" only "if we hold the beginning of our confidence steadfast unto the end."

Particularly do these events speak to those living in the days of the final crisis of history when "the love of many" will again "wax cold," and only a remnant will stand firm and true. God grant that in that day we, like Peter, may be so "sure" of Jesus and His purpose for our lives that we may hold fast through the darkest hour and be "with Him" in the day of His glory and triumph.

This chapter is based on John 6:25-7:1.

Real Religion

THE rulers in Jerusalem expected that Jesus would come up to the capital for the feast of the Passover, and had laid new plans to silence Him. But knowing their evil designs, He did not go. Instead He remained in the neighbourhood of Capernaum, teaching and healing all who came to Him. When, therefore, the feast was over the Pharisees deputed some of their number to go into Galilee to harass Jesus there.

In the eyes of the Pharisees the most serious charge against Jesus was His open neglect of the rules and regulations of the oral law or "law upon the lip" which they claimed had been given by God as a supplement to the written law. These oral laws had been gathered together by the rabbinical schools into the Talmud, comprising the Mishna, or added law, and the Gemara, a commentary upon it, and these were regarded as not merely of equal, but of even greater authority than the written law.

If the Scriptures were compared to water, they said, the Mishna was as wine, while the Gemara was as special wine. It was a "greater offence to teach anything contrary to the voice of the rabbis than to contradict Scripture itself." And to set Scripture against the authority of "tradition" was actually to risk the loss of a place in the kingdom of God.

No wonder, therefore, that Jesus took every opportunity to discountenance the man-made "tradition of the elders" and to exalt the authority of the pure Word of God.

The spies from Jerusalem found Jesus, as usual, surrounded by a crowd seeking healing and instruction, and immediately they launched into their attack. Fearing to accuse Him personally, in the presence of His fellow Galileans, they challenged Him through His disciples.

The Pharisees and Herodians plotting together to destroy Jesus.
By J. J. TISSOT

"Why," they demanded, "do Thy disciples transgress the tradition of the elders? for they wash not their hands when they eat bread."

By this they did not mean that the disciples failed to observe the simple requirements of cleanliness, but that they did not meticulously perform the numerous ceremonial ablutions required by the Talmudic law. Actually, one whole book of the oral law dealt with rules for washing on rising, washing after return from market, washing before and after meals, before prayers, and on countless other occasions. Sometimes the fingers only needed to be washed; at other times the washing was ordered up to the wrists or the elbows. In certain circumstances the washing movement was upward, in others it was downward. Sometimes the water was poured onto the hands; at other times one fist was rubbed vigorously into the other palm.

There were equally minute rules for the washing of domestic vessels, couches, and so on, with appropriate prayers to go with them, so much so that the Sadducees used to say that the Pharisees would give the sun a washing if they could!

By accusing the disciples of failing to observe all these multifarious rules, the Pharisees hoped to get Jesus to make some disparaging remark about the rabbinical law which they could use against Him. But Jesus declined to argue. Instead He faced them with a far more serious counter-accusation: "Why do ye also transgress the commandment of God by your tradition?"

By way of illustration, He went on, "For God commanded, saying, Honour thy father and mother: and, He that curseth father or mother, let him die the death. But ye say, whosoever shall say to his father or his mother, It is Corban [that is, a gift intended for the Corbana, or sacred treasury of the temple] . . . he shall be free" from any responsibility to help them.

This was a particularly hypocritical evasion of the responsibilities of the fifth commandment, for such a dedication did not involve the immediate devotion of the gift to the temple. The donor was permitted to make personal use of it during his lifetime provided it was deeded to the temple at his death. Thus both God and the parents were cheated, and the commandment, intended to foster filial affection, was made of "none effect" by their "tradition."

"Ye hypocrites," Jesus declared, "well did Esaias prophesy of you, saying, This people draweth nigh unto Me with their mouth, and honoureth Me with their lips; but their heart is far from Me. But in vain they do worship Me, teaching for doctrines the commandments of men."

Superficially they acted as if their supreme desire was to honour God and obey His will, but beneath this veneer of religiosity their hearts were selfish and evil.

Turning from the Pharisees to the crowd, Jesus completed His exposure of their sham piety as He cried, "Hearken unto Me every one of you, and understand: There is nothing from without a man, that entering into him can defile him: but the things which come out of him, those are they that defile the man."

The Pharisees were furious that Jesus should have so humiliated them before the people and hurried off, leaving Jesus to return with His disciples to the house where they lodged. When they were alone the disciples began to question the wisdom of publicly denouncing such influential men. "Knowest Thou that the Pharisees were offended, after they heard this saying?" they said to Him with some alarm.

"Let them alone," Jesus replied. "Every plant, which My heavenly Father hath not planted, shall be rooted up. . . . They be blind leaders of the blind. And if the blind lead the blind, both shall fall into the ditch."

But Peter still was not satisfied. What did Jesus mean by the parable He spoke to the people, "Not that which goeth into the mouth defileth a man; but that which cometh out of a man, this defileth a man"?

"Are ye also yet without understanding?" Jesus asked in reply to his further question. "Do not ye perceive, that whatsoever thing from without entereth into the man, it cannot defile him; because it entereth not into his heart, but into the belly" and ultimately "goeth out."

But "from within, out of the heart of men, proceed evil thoughts, adulteries, fornications, murders, thefts, covetousness, wickedness, deceit, lasciviousness, an evil eye, blasphemy, pride, foolishness. . . . These are the things which defile a man: but to eat with unwashen hands defileth not a man."

The rabbis multiplied rules to ensure that no defilement should remain upon them, and they complicated the law of clean and unclean meats by many supplementary requirements to make sure that they ate nothing having any taint of uncleanness, but they took no precautions to rid themselves of evil thoughts or suppress the criticisms and lying slanders which they allowed to pass their lips. If their hearts had been pure they would not have needed to fear any external contamination.

An outward correctness which bears no relation to the condition of the inner life is not merely useless; it is wicked. Man may be deceived by outward profession, but God knows what is "in man" and judges by the state of the heart.

In the spiritual darkness of the Middle Ages the papal priesthood, like the Pharisees, demanded obedience to the tradition of the church, while neglecting the great principles of the Gospel, and it was against the hollow ceremonialism of Rome that the Reformers protested, and sought to restore the true emphasis upon purity of heart and personal holiness. The continued need of this emphasis today is evident when we note the prophetic denunciation of the outstanding sins of the last days. "This know also," declares the apostle Paul, "that in the last days perilous times shall come. For men shall be lovers of their own selves, covetous, boasters, proud, blasphemers, disobedient to parents, unthankful, unholy, without natural affection, trucebreakers, false accusers, incontinent, fierce, despisers of those that are good; . . . having a form of godliness, but denying the power thereof."

Such are the manifestations of spiritual Phariseeism in our day against which we must be on our guard and from which we are exhorted resolutely to "turn away."

The only true religion is that which proceeds from a heart cleansed and renewed by the saving grace of God and which expresses itself in an outward life in conformity to the will and law of God.

This chapter is based on John 7:1-23; Matthew 15:1-20.

A Heathen Woman's Faith

THE bitter controversy with the Pharisees from Jerusalem convinced Jesus that there would be no more peace for Him by the shores of Galilee, and so, some time in the late spring of A.D. 30, He set off northward over the hills with His disciples, quite likely along the road through the mountain town of Sepphoris, toward the borders of the Roman province of Phœnicia. In some secluded frontier town, inhabited by a mixed population of heathen and Jews, He found refuge, hoping to be left alone for a little while.

Apart from His need of rest and quiet, there was something symbolic in this journey, for, with His earthly ministry moving on to its close, it was as if He was turning His back upon Israel and lifting His eyes toward the regions beyond where the Gospel had yet to go.

As He looked down from the hills upon the Phœnician plain and the busy trading cities of Tyre and Sidon, twenty miles or so away, He must have thought of the time when the Gospel would be carried along the great Roman roads and the sea lanes of commerce to the ends of the inhabited earth. And while He was there an incident occurred which gave the disciples a glimpse of the wider ministry in which they soon were to be engaged.

It was too much to hope that, even in this remote spot, Jesus could "be hid" for very long. Among the crowds which had followed Him in Lower Galilee there had been many from the border regions of Tyre and Sidon, and they had taken back to their towns and villages news of the Miracle-worker of Capernaum. A very short time, therefore, after His arrival Jesus was recognized by at least one needy soul.

As He walked with His disciples in the village a woman approached and threw

---

In a border town in Northern Galilee a Syro-phœnician woman came to Jesus to plead for the healing of her daughter.

By W. G. SIMMONDS

herself at His feet, pleading His help on behalf of her daughter who was possessed of an unclean spirit.

The woman was not a Jew, but a heathen of the ancient Phœnician race. There is a tradition, recorded by Tatian, that she came from the city of Homs, but the Bible simply calls her a Syrophœnician woman, that is, a Phœnician of Syria in contrast to the North African Phœnicians of Carthage.

By religion she was a worshipper of Baal or Ashteroth, and doubtless had spent much of her means seeking the ministrations of the heathen priests. But it had been all to no avail, and when she heard that the Galilean Healer was in the vicinity she determined to seek His aid.

Her cry as He passed by, "Have mercy on me, O Lord, Thou Son of David," shows that word had reached even this remote village that Jesus the Miracle-worker was none other than the Messiah of prophecy and David's greater Son. But though the woman cried loudly after Jesus He walked on unheeding, apparently absorbed in His meditations.

The disciples knew that He had come up into the hills for quiet, and interpreted His silence as an indication that He did not want to attract attention by working any miracle in that place. It seemed to them, however, that if she persisted in crying after Him she would precipitate the kind of disturbance He was anxious to avoid, so they suggested that He might do something for her and then "send her away."

Jesus knew quite well what He was going to do, but first He wanted to test the prejudices of the disciples and the persistence of this heathen woman. So in her hearing He said to the disciples, "I am not sent but to the lost sheep of the house of Israel."

Now it was quite true that Jesus had come in the first place to "His own," and when He sent out the twelve on their first missionary journey He expressly told them not to go into any Gentile or even Samaritan city. But this did not mean that He would not bestow His blessing upon any Gentile who came to Him in his or her need. They had, in fact, seen Him answer the appeal of the centurion for the healing of his trusted servant. Jesus spoke like this to see whether the disciples had shed their national exclusiveness sufficiently to plead her cause.

The reaction of the disciples to Jesus' remark is not recorded but the woman was in no way daunted by the apparent rebuff. Running after Jesus, she prostrated herself in an attitude of worship, and pleaded, "Lord, help me." Even if she had no right to invoke Him as "Son of David," she believed she could come to Him as the "Lord" of all mankind and, on this ground, she renewed her plea for His help.

Still Jesus seemed to refuse her any encouragement. "Let the children first be filled," He replied: "for it is not meet to take the children's bread, and to cast it unto the dogs."

Strange words these surely seem from the lips of Jesus! A Pharisee would have had no compunction in calling this heathen woman a dog, but Jesus could hardly be expected to speak in this way.

Actually, what Jesus said was not callous and disdainful as it might appear. The woman was quick to notice that He did not refer to her as a loathsome "cur," as a bigoted Jew might have done, but that He used an affectionate term which meant a "little pet dog." Pet dogs were not often found in Jewish homes, but they were quite common in Greek houses. They were allowed access to the family rooms and during meals would sit beneath the table waiting for discarded scraps.

The phrasing of Jesus' reply told the woman that, though she was not of the house of Israel, she was nevertheless an object of love and care. Eagerly, therefore, she took Him at His word. She might have no claim to sit at the table as a daughter of Israel, but as a "little pet dog" she was quite prepared to wait under the table to "eat of the children's crumbs" which fell to the ground. She asked only to be treated with the favour which would be extended to a pet dog and to receive such "crumbs" of blessing as Jesus had for her.

How ready Jesus was to respond to her plea. Too often He had had the experience of the natural children ungratefully casting away the "Bread of life." How then could He refuse one who, in poverty of spirit, asked only for a share of the "crumbs"?

Gently raising her from the ground Jesus said earnestly, "O woman, great is thy faith." Only on one other occasion had Jesus commended an individual for "great" faith and that, strangely enough, was the Gentile centurion.

"For this saying," He continued, "go thy way; the devil is gone out of thy daughter."

Gratefully the woman hurried off and "when she was come to her house, she found the devil gone out," and her daughter lying quietly upon her bed. A "crumb" of divine power had been more than sufficient to destroy Satan's hold upon her.

To the disciples this miracle was a wonderful object lesson of the wideness of divine love. They had seen Jesus break down the false barriers between Jew and Samaritan when He brought salvation to the woman at the well of Sychar. They had noted His ready response to the appeal of the believing Roman centurion. Now they saw Him exerting His power on behalf of a heathen Gentile as freely as for an Israelite after the flesh.

It was not easy for the disciples to shed the idea, which had been inculcated into their minds by their national leaders, that Israel only were entitled to the interest and care of God, and still more lessons would be needed before they fully realized that, in respect of grace, there was "no difference between the Jew and the Greek," and that "the same Lord over all is rich unto all that call upon Him." This acted parable on the borders of the great Gentile world was one of the experiences preparing them for the day when Jesus would send them forth to make disciples of all nations, and gather them into His church where there would be "neither Jew nor Greek . . . bond nor free . . . male nor female," but in which all would be "one in Christ Jesus."

This chapter is based on Matthew 15:21-28; Mark 7:24-30.

The Great Detour

SOON after He had healed the daughter of the Syrophœnician woman, Jesus left His mountain retreat. Not wishing yet to return to the hostile atmosphere of Capernaum He turned north-eastward with His disciples up the deep valley of the Orontes, crossed the southern spurs of the Lebanon range, and descended into the "hollow of Syria" between the Lebanon and Anti-Lebanon Mountains, near where the Jordan rises.

Following the right bank of the stream the little company skirted the reedy marshes of Lake Huleh, called in the Old Testament the "Waters of Merom," and crossed the Jordan most likely at the Bridge of the Daughters of Jacob, so called because the patriarch's caravan, travelling in the opposite direction long before, re-entered Canaan here from Mesopotamia.

Over the bridge, Jesus and the disciples traversed the uplands of Gaulanitis, the province of the tetrarch Philip, and once more reached the hilly eastern shore of the Sea of Galilee after a journey of something like a hundred and twenty miles from the border region of Phœnicia.

Though they travelled quietly and Jesus had worked no miracles among the Gentiles, by the time they reached the lake shore a considerable multitude had gathered. Some, no doubt, had followed Jesus all the way from northern Galilee, but many were Gentiles of the Decapolis, who had first heard of Jesus from the healed demoniacs of Gergesa.

As Jesus sat talking with His disciples in a quiet spot by the lake, a poor deaf mute was brought forward by friends who asked Jesus to restore his hearing and speech. As He looked upon the afflicted man Jesus "sighed," not because His rest had been disturbed, but in compassion, so pitiable and impotent did he seem. Perhaps

---

As soon as it was known that Jesus was passing by, a stream of lame and maimed, blind and dumb, came to Him for help.   By J. J. TISSOT

Jesus also saw in him a symbol of sin's deadening effects upon the spiritual nature of man.

To avoid exciting the multitude, Jesus drew the man aside a little way. Then, moistening His finger, He touched the man's ears and tongue as if to encourage him, through the sense of touch, to believe.

Expectantly the man looked up at Jesus and, as He pronounced the words, "Be opened," he felt his ears become unstopped, his vocal chords loosen, and immediately he both heard and spoke.

The miracle might have passed unobserved if the healed man and his friends had obeyed Jesus' injunction to say nothing about it to anyone. But they could not keep such joy to themselves, and soon a stream of lame and maimed, blind and dumb, were making their way to Him, and all who came in simple trust, whether Jew or Gentile, were healed.

In wonder and amazement the crowd watched as they saw the eyes of the blind opened, the lame stand to their feet, the dumb speak, and they glorified the God of Israel who had sent this Miracle-worker among them. "He hath done all things well," they exclaimed.

When night came, Jesus and His disciples slept on the hillside under the open sky and the next day He again healed all who came to Him. On the third day the crowds still showed no signs of diminishing. By this time, the little stocks of food which the people had brought in their pouches had gone and they began to realize how far it was to the cities where they could buy more. But the crisis did not take Jesus unawares. He could have sent the people away while they still had enough food to last till they reached home. But He deliberately continued His ministry to this largely Gentile multitude that He might manifest His power not only as the Healer of their diseases, but as the Satisfier of their every need, temporal and spiritual. So, as alarm began to spread among the people by reason of the shortage of provisions, Jesus called His disciples and said to them, "I have compassion on the multitude, because they have now been with Me three days, and have nothing to eat."

The disciples, of course, remembered what Jesus had done for a Jewish multitude not long before, and not so very far away, but, blinded still by their long-held prejudices, they could not believe that He would do this as readily for Gentiles. So instead of reminding Him of His earlier miracle they replied, "From whence can a man satisfy these men with bread here in the wilderness?"

Jesus knew from their question that they did not expect, or even

When all the multitude were fed no fewer than seven large basketsful of fragments were gathered up.   By DUBUFE

want Him to miraculously feed these Gentiles, but He did not reprove them. Instead, He followed precisely the same pattern of action as when He fed the five thousand.

"How many loaves have ye?" He asked.

When they heard this familiar question it began to dawn upon their minds that Jesus was going to repeat His former miracle. Hurriedly they made inquiries and came back with the word that they had found "seven" loaves and "a few little fishes" of the same kind that the little boy had had in his satchel. This time they did not say, "What are they among so many?" for they knew from experience that few or many were all the same to Jesus.

At His bidding the disciples once again assembled the multitude into groups and then gathered around Jesus. As on the former occasion, Jesus took the loaves and fishes and asked a blessing over them. Then, as He began to divide the food, they saw it again multiply in His hands. And at His command they carried the laden baskets from group to group among the people until all "were filled."

When the meal was over they did not need any bidding to pick up their baskets and gather the surplus food. But great was their amazement when they filled not just twelve small travellers' pouches as on the former occasion, but seven large wicker hampers big enough to hold a man.

It was one more reminder that all men everywhere, Gentile as well as Jew, are equally the subjects of His love and the recipients of His grace.

This chapter is based on Matthew 15:32-39; Mark 7:31-8:10.

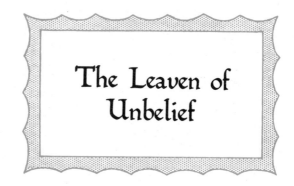

CHAPTER
SEVENTY

The Leaven of Unbelief

AFTER the second miracle of the loaves and fishes the crowd dispersed quietly. On this occasion there was no agitation like that after the feeding of the five thousand, for the multitude here was largely Gentile and their interest in Jesus was as a heaven-sent Healer and Teacher rather than as the expected Messiah and King.

When the people had gone Jesus entered into a waiting boat and set off with His disciples across the lake to the Galilean side. They did not make straight for Capernaum but, on the instructions of Jesus, directed the boat toward Magdala about half-way down the west side of the lake, represented today by the poor Arab village of Majdel.

Mark's reference to "Dalmanutha" as the place where they landed, has led some to think that they had sailed down to the south end of the lake where there is a place still called Ed Delhemijah, but it is more likely that Dalmanutha was a name given to the little plain around Magdala where the Valley of Doves opens out as it reaches the lake.

Jesus may have chosen to land quietly here rather than at populous Capernaum in order to avoid further conflict with the rulers of the Jews, but no sooner was His return reported, than the Pharisees, in company with Sadducees and Herodians, "came forth, and began to question with Him." The Pharisees most likely had arrived post haste from Capernaum, while the Sadducees and Herodians could have come up the coast from Herod's lakeside capital, Tiberias.

That adherents of these two rival Jewish factions had now joined forces to challenge Jesus is a striking indication of the universal enmity against Jesus among the leaders of the nation, for the Pharisees and Sadducees represented both political

Not wishing to attract a crowd Jesus led the blind man of Bethsaida out of the town to a quiet place and there restored his sight.   By CARL BLOCH

and theological extremes, and were in nearly everything else bitterly opposed to one another.

The Pharisees were intensely nationalistic, hating the Romans and the Herods equally, while the Sadducees and Herodians had secured the highest offices in church and state by currying favour with the foreign rulers.

The Pharisees demanded meticulous observance of all the minutiæ of the rabbinical law, while the sceptical Sadducees cared little for the hair-splitting of the traditionalists.

The Pharisees were ascetics, while the Sadducees were worldly, luxury-loving, and lax alike in morals and in religious observance.

But though they were at opposite poles in religion and politics, they were at one in their intense hatred of Jesus. The Pharisees were angered because He was undermining respect for their "traditions." The Sadducees hated Him because they feared He might start a rebellion which would expel their patrons, the Herods, and oust them from political and ecclesiastical power.

So here at Magdala, for the first time in the Gospel record, these erstwhile enemies joined forces to oppose Jesus. Gathering menacingly around Him they demanded that He give evidence of His divine authority by showing them a "sign from heaven."

In the mouths of the sceptical Sadducees the demand was a sneer at all professed supernatural authority, and voiced by the Pharisees it revealed how completely they had failed to understand the Messianic prophecies of the Old Testament. These Jewish leaders were looking so anxiously for Messiah the King that they did not recognize the "servant of Jehovah" who came to make known the love of God to man and to pay with His life the price of human redemption. They were watching so intently for heavenly signs of the kingdom of glory that they missed the earthly signs of the coming of the kingdom of grace into their midst.

The prophet Daniel had declared that "from the going forth of the commandment to restore and to build Jerusalem," after the return from Babylonian captivity, "unto the Messiah" would be sixty-nine weeks of years. At the very time when this period of 483 years expired in A.D. 27, Jesus came into Galilee "preaching the Gospel of the kingdom of God, and saying, The time is fulfilled, and the kingdom of God is at hand: repent ye, and believe the Gospel."

At His birth, thirty years before, the glad tidings were proclaimed by the shepherds who were divinely led to His manger, by the wise men who came from a far country to worship Him, and by Simeon and Anna in the temple, but all these Messianic "signs" they had dismissed as without significance.

The appearance of Jesus in Judea was immediately preceded by the preaching of John the Baptist in exact fulfilment of the prophetic Word, and John had testified that Jesus was "the Lamb of God."

The teaching of Jesus and His accompanying miracles likewise incontestibly identified Him as the Coming One, whom the prophets had described in such detail.

There had actually been an abundance of "signs from heaven," such as the angels' song, the descent of the Dove, and the testimony of God at Jesus' baptism, but all were set aside and ignored. Little wonder, therefore, that when they asked Jesus for a further sign He sternly reproved them for the blindness of their proud hearts.

The Pharisees made great profession of their ability to read and interpret the physical "signs" in the heavens. In the evening they would look up at the sky and say, "It will be fair weather: for the sky is red." In the morning they would go out of the house and say, "It will be foul weather today: for the sky is red and lowring."

When the clouds hung low over Mount Hermon they would prophesy rain and they knew the signs of the coming of the dry sorocco winds from the eastern desert. They claimed even to predict from the appearance of the smoke which rose from the temple at the Feast of Tabernacles what the weather for the ensuing months would be. If it turned north they forecast much rain, if south a dry season. If it turned east all would be well; if west the whole land would mourn.

Of all this weather lore, which at best was of merely temporal value, the Pharisees made great boast, but to the spiritual signs of the Messiah, for which they were supposed to be on the watch, they were completely blind.

"O ye hypocrites," Jesus declared, "Ye can discern the face of the sky; but can ye not discern the signs of the times?"

"A wicked and adulterous generation seeketh" after another sign, He went on, but no sign would be given to it except one for which it had not asked, "the sign of the prophet Jonas." They were looking for a mighty King who would destroy their enemies and usher Israel into His kingdom; but God was sending them a Jonah message to warn them that if they did not turn from their transgressions judgment would fall upon them. If they repented like the Ninevites they would find God as merciful as He was to that city, but if they did not, destruction would not tarry long.

"The men of Nineveh shall rise in judgment with this generation, and shall condemn it," Jesus said even more pointedly on another occasion: "because they repented" at the preaching of Jonas; "and, behold, a greater than Jonas is here."

There was another meaning to this "sign of the prophet Jonah" which was later to emerge. For as Jonah was "three days" in the body of the great fish before his deliverance, so the crowning sign that Jesus was the Messiah would be His glorious resurrection after "three days and three nights in the heart of the earth."

This latter meaning the Jews could not have appreciated at the time and they were too proud to recognize any connection between the Ninevites and themselves. Furious at His insinuation, but unable to frame any effective reply, they turned their backs upon Him and departed.

This encounter convinced Jesus that He could accomplish nothing with the leaders of the Jews dogging His footsteps everywhere He went. So, turning with His disciples to their waiting boat, they sailed away northward along the lake shore.

As they passed Capernaum the disciples must have looked longingly at the clustered houses which came right down to the water's edge, for it was several months since

they had seen their homes and kindred. But Jesus bade them sail on and soon they were disembarking at the north end of the lake not far from the place where the five thousand were fed.

Jesus had said little on the voyage, for His heart was saddened by the increasing hatred of the Jewish leaders, but when His disciples gathered around Him on the beach to learn His plans He said to them, "Take heed and beware of the leaven of the Pharisees and of the Sadducees."

For a moment the disciples thought that Jesus was admonishing them not to buy food from any Pharisee or Sadducee, for in their haste, they had failed to bring any provisions for the journey. But as they were whispering among themselves Jesus broke in, "Why reason ye among yourselves, because ye have brought no bread? Do ye not . . . remember the five loaves of the five thousand, and how many baskets ye took up? Neither the seven loaves of the four thousand, and how many baskets ye took up?"

Then the disciples understood that He was not speaking of material bread, but was warning them against the "doctrine of the Pharisees and of the Sadducees," for these two leading sects of the Jews typified the conditions of mind and heart which were rendering so many blind to the "present truth" for their times.

The Pharisees were so absorbed in the observance of ceremonial rules and regulations that they failed to recognize in Jesus the fount of grace and truth. The Sadducees were so deeply influenced by the scepticism of the heathen philosophies of their time, that they questioned any alleged manifestation of the supernatural. While the Herodian Sadducees, as their name suggests, were so fully occupied in currying favour with the house of Herod and their Roman masters in order to satisfy their aspirations for wealth, position, and power, that they were utterly heedless of the spiritual riches which Christ sought to confer upon them. In consequence the Pharisees, Sadducees, and Herodians all failed to recognize the movings of Providence among them until too late.

By comparing the externalism of the Pharisees and the secularism of the Sadducees and Herodians to the potency of leaven Jesus was emphasizing the danger of permitting either to gain the least foothold in their hearts. For as leaven quickly "leaveneth the whole lump," so will such traits spread their evil influence and subvert heart and life from the way of holiness.

In the past nineteen hundred years human hearts have changed little and the mental and spiritual characteristics of the Pharisees, Sadducees, and Herodians are still all too common. The apostle Paul declared that, in the last days, many would be satisfied with "a form of godliness" and have no desire for the "power" of the Gospel in their lives. And there are all too many such spiritual Pharisees in our time.

Modern Sadduceeism finds expression in the increasing modernism of our day which sets the so-called "assured" findings of science against the revealed truths of the Bible.

And are not the position-seeking Herodians represented by multitudes whose lives are spent in a vain quest for worldly wealth, position, and influence to the neglect of the spiritual treasures of grace and fellowship with Christ and His people?

So the urgent counsel of Jesus comes down to His disciples in our day to "beware" of worldly associations, the inordinate love of possessions, position, and power, empty formalism, and all the "philosophy and vain deceit" antagonistic to God's revelation to men. For, once permitted entrance to heart and mind they will, like leaven, spread their pernicious poison through the whole being, "spoiling" the experience, "hardening" the heart, and turning the soul from its heavenly quest.

And if further reinforcement of the words of Jesus be needed, we have only to ponder the tragic example of Judas, who, by tolerating the evil leaven of unholy ambition in his heart, made shipwreck of his experience and consummated his treachery by becoming the instrument of the betrayal and death of Christ.

Only by submitting to the divine purging of our lives of every trace of the leaven of hypocrisy, unrighteousness, and unbelief, can we be preserved "blameless" until the day when the Lord shall come to claim His own.

This chapter is based on Matthew 16:1-12; Mark 8:11-21.

Jesus and His disciples rest beneath the trees on the slopes of Mount Hermon, near Cæsarea Philippi.
By J. J. TISSOT

CHAPTER SEVENTY-ONE

The Keys of the Kingdom

JESUS and His disciples were passing through Bethsaida Julias on their way north in search of quiet amid the growing storm of opposition, when a blind man was brought to Him. Not wishing to attract a crowd, Jesus quietly took the man by the hand and led him out of the town.

When they reached a secluded spot Jesus moistened His fingers upon His tongue and rubbed them over the gummed eyelids of the blind man. He then asked him if he could see anything. After a moment the man replied, "I see men as trees, walking." He was conscious of shadows passing before his eyes which he knew to be men, but which looked more like the trees he had seen in the sighted days of his youth. Again Jesus put His hands over the man's eyes and when He took them away the second time, he could see clearly.

Jesus had healed many blind men before, but this miracle was unique in that the man's recovery took place, not instantaneously, but in two distinct stages. Clearly, there was some reason for Jesus working in this way. It may be that the man at first had no personal faith and only came because he was induced to do so by his friends. If so, the first partial miracle was intended to change his unbelief into eager faith and then, in response to his ardent desire, he was rewarded by complete healing.

Is not that how our merciful Saviour so often deals with the spiritually blind? Into their darkness He sends the first glimmer of the light of truth. Then, as awakened faith finds expression in a desire for transformation of life, more light is given until at last the soul is walking in the full light of the Gospel of God.

Actually, of course, however responsive our spiritual faculties may be, we can, in this life, know only "in part." At best, as the apostle Paul says, we now see through the glass only "darkly," or indistinctly, like the blind man in the first stage of his

---

As spokesmen of the disciples Peter confesses their faith in Jesus as "the Christ, the Son of the living God."

By GLOETZLE

recovery. But if we faithfully walk in the light that God vouchsafes to us on earth, we shall assuredly one day know as we are known. The imperfect vision and understanding of earth will merge into the perfect vision of heaven.

Telling the restored man to go straight back to his home and to make no mention of the miracle till He had gone, Jesus slipped quietly away and continued His journey northward. At last He reached the region of Cæsarea Philippi, the chief city of Iturea, in the shadow of mighty Hermon, the highest peak of the Anti-Lebanon Mountains.

An intriguing tradition suggests that Jesus was given hospitality by the woman who was healed in Capernaum by touching the hem of His garment, but as it was now around midsummer, it is more likely that He and His disciples found shelter in the thick woods which clothed the lower slopes of the mountain range.

It was as beautiful a spot as could be found anywhere in the Palestine of Jesus' day. At the foot of the hill upon which the city stood the waters of the River Jordan flowed out from a cave in the limestone cliff. Now the roof of the cave has fallen in, and countless little streamlets gush forth between the boulders and fallen stones and plunge down a narrow gorge to join another torrent, the Nahr el Leddan, from Tel el Kadi across the valley.

In the rocks around the cave mouth are many carved niches which once contained marble statues of naiads of the stream and dryads of the woods, for in these sylvan glades Pan, the nature god of the Greeks, was worshipped. In those days this natural temple was called the Paneion after the heathen diety, while the district bore the name of Paneas. In some of the niches around the mouth of the cavern the name of the god is still recognizable.

When the district was given by the Roman Emperor Augustus to Herod the Great about A.D. 20, the Idumean king rebuilt the city, renamed it Cæsarea, and erected a white marble temple containing a statue of the "divine" Augustus. The remains of the strong wall and massive towers which enclosed the Herodian city may be represented by the ruins which now overlook the modern village and its fields.

When Herod's son, Philip, took over the tetrarchy of Trachonitis he beautified the earlier town and called it Cæsarea Philippi to distinguish it from the Cæsarea his father had built on the Palestine coast south of Carmel. King Agrippa II changed its name again to Neronias, after the infamous Emperor Nero, but with the decline of the Roman Empire it reverted to its old Greek name of Banias. Today a Moslem shrine and the ruins of a Crusader castle are added to the remains of the might of Rome and the sensual nature emblems of the Greeks.

Jesus brought His disciples to this remote region primarily to be away from the ever-pressing multitudes and out of sight of the prying eyes of His enemies, but He could not have chosen a more striking setting in which to establish their faith in Him and announce His redemptive purpose.

Sitting doubtless within sight of the symbols of the great pagan religions of His day, Jesus began by asking the disciples what they had heard concerning Him as they moved about among the people. "Whom do men say that I the Son of man am?"

"Some," the disciples at once answered, "say that Thou art John the Baptist." Herod himself was one who feared that this might be so, and that he had been raised from the dead specifically to bring judgment upon his wicked murderer.

Others, they said, thought that He was "Elias," for Malachi declared that the prophet who had been carried up to heaven in a chariot of fire would come back again to herald the "Messenger of the covenant."

Still others had suggested that He might be "Jeremias," or one of the other prophets of Israel.

Jesus, of course, knew before He asked that He had been identified with all these men of earlier days, but He let the disciples mention them all in order to lead up to His next question: "But whom say ye that I am?"

From the beginning of His ministry the disciples of Jesus had confessed their belief that He was the Messiah and on more than one occasion they had offered worship to Him as the divine Son of God. When many of His followers turned from Him in disappointment because He did not fit into the popular conception of Messiah, the twelve had whole-heartedly associated themselves with Peter's confident affirmation, "We believe and are sure that Thou art that Christ, the Son of the living God." Now again, in response to Jesus' plain question, Peter, without hesitation, voices their unswerving faith. "Thou art the Christ, the Son of the living God."

Jesus wanted His disciples to confess their faith in His divine Sonship at this time, for only as they truly recognized this would they be able to understand the vicarious and atoning significance of the death He was soon to die and the nature of the redemption which He was to send them forth to proclaim.

Immediately this fundamental declaration of faith had been spoken by Peter on behalf of the disciples Jesus earnestly responded, "Blessed art thou, Simon Bar-jona: for flesh and blood hath not revealed it unto thee, but My Father which is in heaven."

Then with a striking play on words He revealed the vital place of that confession and the one who bore it in the establishment of His church and kingdom.

"I say also unto thee," He declared, "That thou art Peter [that is, a stone], and upon this rock [of which you have given evidence that you are a part] I will build My church: and the gates of hell shall not prevail against it."

As He spoke, Jesus may well have looked up at the massive walls and towers of Cæsarea Philippi crowning the craggy hill. These represented the might of the greatest earthly empire the world had ever seen, but the church's foundation would be more solid and unshakable than the strongest fortress of Rome, for not even the great adversary behind the "gates of hell" would be able to muster power sufficient to prevail against it. Indeed, Satan would be impotent to resist the entrance of Christ when He should burst its gates to release his captives.

How truly Jesus spoke is evident today, for while upon and around the hill on which Cæsarea Philippi stood are only the broken ruins of mighty Rome, the message born of Peter's great confession has gone on its conquering way into all the earth to make disciples of every nation.

OPPOSITE

Near the source of the
Jordan in Upper Galil[e]

ABOVE

The Crusader castle w[
once defended the an[
port of Sidon.

LEFT

Fishing nets hung up to [
along the harbour qua[
Sidon.

What a tragedy it is, however, that this tremendous statement of Jesus should have been so perverted by one particular section of Christendom, that it should advance the claim to be the church of Peter and to possess exclusive apostolic authority over all Christians, when there is not a shred of evidence for this arrogant contention.

It needed a Rock *(petra)* to provide a foundation for the church, but however rock-like Peter might have been at that moment he was at best only a piece of rock, or a stone *(petros)*. The great Rock upon which the church is built is time and again revealed in the prophetic Scriptures to be Christ Himself. Both Peter and Paul attributed the prophecies of the "Rock" to Christ, while confessing themselves to be "lively stones" built on the divine foundation.

If Jesus had, at this time, pronounced Peter chief of the apostles, surely all the gospel writers would have recorded the momentous declaration, but actually the incident is only set down by Matthew. Again, it is hardly likely that James and John would have aspired to the highest place in the future kingdom if they knew that this position had already been given to Peter. And surely Paul would have been more discreet than publicly to have resisted Peter "to the face because he was to be blamed," over the issue of circumcision, if he were the divinely appointed head of the church on earth.

Furthermore, if Jesus had given Peter primacy over the church, he and not James would have presided at the first council in Jerusalem referred to in the fifteenth chapter of Acts. The facts are, however, that Peter never claimed leadership in the church, nor was it ever accorded to him by the disciples. None of the early church fathers makes use of this text to give pre-eminence to the bishop of Rome, nor is any such affirmation included in any early creed or article of faith. Neither Augustine, one of the greatest theologians of the Latin church, nor Jerome, the translator of the Latin Vulgate, held such an exclusive view. In point of fact, not until the late fifth century was Christ's declaration to Peter appropriated by Pope Leo I to support his claim that the bishop of Rome was primate of all Christendom.

Continuing His declaration to Peter as spokesman and representative of the disciples, Jesus went on to outline the church's future task. "And I will give unto thee the keys of the kingdom of heaven: and whatsoever thou shalt bind on earth shall be bound in heaven: and whatsoever thou shalt loose on earth shall be loosed in heaven."

These words, of course, are claimed by Rome as further evidence that Peter was thereby appointed to primacy among the apostles and the supreme authority in the church, but this was far from Christ's meaning.

Because God had committed to Israel the sacred "oracles," the Pharisees frequently spoke of their authority to "bind" and "loose" in dispensing the things of God to men.

Jesus condemned the rulers of the Jews because they had failed to use the "key of knowledge" to gain entrance to the kingdom of grace themselves, and had prevented those who desired to use it from doing so. And because they had proved their utter unworthiness to hold the "keys of the kingdom," Jesus committed them to the apostles. Henceforth they were to act as the doorkeepers of the kingdom.

As the spokesman of the church, Peter began to exercise "the power of the keys" at Pentecost when, through his witness, three thousand souls were admitted into the fold of the church. Later, he was used to admit Cornelius and the first Gentile converts, as well as to shut the door against Simon Magus who had "neither part nor lot" in the kingdom.

But he was not the only one to exercise this authority. The other disciples continued the work he began and Paul, by divine ordination, was the apostle chiefly responsible for opening wide the doors of the kingdom to the Gentiles.

Jesus used exactly the same words that He spoke to Peter in addressing the whole company of the disciples on a later occasion, and after His resurrection He gave equal authority to all the disciples assembled in the upper room: "Whose soever sins ye remit," He told them, "they are remitted unto them; and whose soever sins ye retain, they are retained." Contrary, therefore, to the hierarchical interpretation of Rome, not only Peter but all the apostles shared equally the "keys" which were to open the kingdom of heaven to men.

If the primacy of Peter among the apostles is thus shown to be baseless and impertinent, the further suggestion that Peter was empowered to pass on his authority and power to his successors in Rome by "apostolic succession" has equally not a shred of evidence in its support. For quite apart from the lack of any biblical evidence for such transference, there is no real proof that Peter was the first bishop of the Christian church in Rome.

The divine plan for the perpetuation of the ministry of the Word is not a mechanical succession. God has not given unconditional authority to any man or church irrespective of their faithfulness to the call of God.

Jesus took this authority away from the religious leaders of the Jews when they ceased to dispense faithfully the oracles of God, and gave it to new spiritual leaders whom He had chosen and prepared for their task.

This transfer of authority was, of course, vigorously contested by the Jewish priesthood, but their continued claims did not in any way affect their rejection. In the same way any section of the Christian church can claim the "apostolic succession" of the Spirit only so long as it remains true to the faith entrusted to it. For this reason we cannot but believe that the true "apostolic succession" passed from the apostate Roman church to the reformers and their successors who restored to the church the Gospel of salvation by faith alone.

Sad to say, however, many of these great churches of the Protestant Reformation are today being transformed into an "image" of apostate Rome from which once they courageously separated. In consequence, we are witnessing the passing of the true succession again to a remnant who are faithfully proclaiming the "present truth" for our time, and who are truly keeping "the commandments of God, and the faith of Jesus."

This chapter is based on Matthew 16:13-20; Mark 8:27-30; Luke 9:18-21.

CHAPTER SEVENTY-TWO

The Shadow of the Cross

O N a number of occasions Jesus had hinted at the path of sorrow and suffering He had come to tread. When the disciples of John asked Him why His disciples did not fast, He replied that while the Bridegroom was with them, the "children of the bridechamber" could only rejoice, but that one day He would be "taken from them," and then they would have cause to fast and mourn.

Comparing Himself, in one of His discourses, to the "Bread of life," He told the unbelieving Jews, "Except ye eat the flesh of the Son of man, and drink His blood, ye have no life in you."

To the ruler Nicodemus, Jesus declared that "as Moses lifted up the serpent in the wilderness, even so must the Son of man be lifted up: that whosoever believeth in Him should not perish, but have eternal life."

All these intimations, however, had been couched in symbolic language which He had not explained to His disciples. Now, in this moment of high faith at Cæsarea Philippi, Jesus began to tell them more plainly than ever before that "He must go unto Jerusalem, and suffer many things of the elders and chief priests and scribes, and be killed."

But, He went on to assure them, this would not mean the failure of His purpose. Rather would it be the prelude to triumph, for on "the third day" He would rise victorious over sin and death to plead the merits of His sacrifice before His Father in heaven.

As Peter was foremost in bearing testimony to his belief in the Messiahship of Jesus, he was the first to express his horror at the path of humiliation which Jesus now revealed would be His lot. He had restrained himself with difficulty when Jesus

---

At Cæsarea Philippi Jesus first spoke plainly to His disciples of His approaching sufferings and death.
By CARL BLOCH

submitted unresistingly to the scorn and opposition of the Pharisees and Sadducees, but he could not be party to allowing his Master's enemies to put Him to death.

Taking hold of Jesus in his anxiety to compel attention to his protest, Peter cried, "Be it far from Thee, Lord: this shall not be unto Thee."

The disciple's outburst was made out of deep love for Jesus and the honour of His cause, but it was a misguided zeal and showed his lack of comprehension of the culminating purpose of Christ's first advent. While he recognized in Jesus the divine Son and the true Messiah, he still failed to understand the relation between the "sufferings of Christ" and the "glory that should follow."

By saying that these things should "not be" he was directly contradicting Jesus who had declared that they "must" be, if man's deliverance from the penalty of sin was to be accomplished.

By his impetuosity he actually allowed Satan to put words into his mouth to turn Jesus from His gracious purpose of redemption.

Detecting the voice of the tempter in Peter's outburst, Jesus turned quickly away saying, "Get thee behind Me, Satan: for thou art an offence unto Me: for thou savourest not the things that be of God, but those that be of men."

In these stern words Jesus did not identify Peter with Satan, but He showed him that, by allowing himself to become a mouthpiece for Satan, he had actually ranged himself with the great adversary in seeking to frustrate the divinely-ordained plan for the salvation of men.

The word "offence" which Jesus chose to describe Peter was a most expressive one, for it was used of the trigger of a trap upon which the bait was placed. Peter had indeed allowed himself to become the bearer of Satan's most subtle temptation to deflect Jesus from His destined way.

Far from being, as papal Rome claims, the "rock" against which Satan would hurl himself in vain, Peter had allowed the "gates of hell" to prevail against him! But from this experience, through the longsuffering of Jesus, Peter learned a profound lesson. And years later, in his letters to the churches, we find the aged apostle untiringly extolling the virtues of the "precious blood of Christ."

"Forasmuch as ye know," he wrote, "that ye were not redeemed with corruptible things, as silver and gold, from your vain conversation, received by tradition from your fathers; but with the precious blood of Christ, as of a Lamb without blemish and without spot: who verily was foreordained before the foundation of the world, but was manifest in these last times for you." What once was unthinkable now aroused his heartfelt gratitude and evoked his dearest love.

Having declared plainly to Peter and the other disciples that His death was essential to the fulfilment of His redemptive mission, Jesus went on to tell them that the "cross" must precede the "crown" in their experience also. "If any man will come after Me," He solemnly declared, "let him deny himself, and take up his cross, and follow Me."

Till now Jesus had not actually disclosed the awful end which awaited Him.

Now they learned the worst, that He would die upon a cruel cross; and that if they loyally followed Him, they must be prepared for a like fate.

Crucifixion was the most terrible form of execution in ancient times. It had been practised by Egyptians, Babylonians, Persians, and Greeks, and under the Romans it was still a common form of punishment meted out to their enemies and for heinous civil offences. Countless Jewish rebels had suffered crucifixion within the memory of the disciples. Invariably it was preceded by scourging, and the victim was then compelled to bear his cross, or at least the upright or crossbeam, to the place of execution.

To accomplish man's redemption Jesus had willingly come to earth to suffer and to die "even the death of the cross." Could His disciples then do less than voluntarily take up their cross and follow in His steps?

But though they might be called upon to sacrifice their all in His cause—home, possessions, family and friends—and to suffer poverty, trial, persecution, and even death, Jesus assured them that the way of the cross would prove, as it would for Him, a path to life and glory.

For paradoxical as it might seem, "whosoever" should seek to save his life by forsaking Him and clinging to the world would ultimately "lose it," while "whosoever" would "lose his life" for Christ's sake, would "find it," eternally.

That self-seeking is self-losing while self-losing Is self-finding will indeed be abundantly manifest when "the Son of man shall come in the glory of His Father with His angels" to reward every man "according to his work." For in that day the glitter of earthly gain will be exposed as false and illusory, while the little crosses Christ's followers have borne will seem as nothing when they take from the hands of the Saviour the "crown of glory" which will be the reward of the righteous.

When Jesus had ended His instruction on the challenge of discipleship He looked into the faces of His little band of followers. They were solemn and anxious and no-one spoke. Even Peter was silent now. But Jesus saw that all except Judas had made their decision. They were ready to follow Him all the way to the cross if thereby they might be counted worthy to live with Him in His kingdom. And so, as He stood in their midst, He made them a striking promise: "Verily I say unto you, There be some standing here, which shall not taste of death, till they see the Son of man coming in His kingdom."

What did Jesus mean by this mysterious promise? He obviously did not mean that some would live to see His return in glory, for all have long since died.

Nor was He referring to His resurrection glory, for not some but all the disciples were witnesses of this.

No, the promise was fulfilled just over a week later on the Mount of Transfiguration when the three most intimate of Christ's disciples were granted a vision, in miniature, of their glorified Lord in order to establish their faith and the confidence of all who afterward should be called upon to follow Jesus along the way of the cross.

This chapter is based on Matthew 16:21-28; Mark 8:31-9:1; Luke 9:22-27.

CHAPTER SEVENTY-THREE

Anticipations of Glory

FROM the solitude of the hills around Cæsarea Philippi, Jesus turned His steps again toward the lake towns of Southern Galilee. The journey which was to end in Jerusalem and on Calvary had begun.

The minds of the disciples were confused by all that Jesus had told them, and their hearts were sad. Jesus had acknowledged the inspired testimony of Peter that He was truly the Messiah for whom Israel looked. Yet He had warned them that very soon He would be taken by His enemies, condemned, and put to death. It was all so different from their anticipations of the triumphant coming of Messiah. And so as they travelled southward they talked among themselves as to what it all meant. But they feared to question Jesus further lest He should reprove their slow understanding.

Just how long Jesus stayed in the region of Cæsarea Philippi after the revelation concerning His future sufferings and death, or how long the little party took on their journey back to Galilee we are not told, but it was some six days after His momentous declaration that, as night was drawing on, Jesus announced to His companions that He was going up into a nearby mountain to pray and would take Peter, James, and John with Him.

His decision aroused no comment from the other disciples for Peter and the two sons of Zebedee had already, by their deeper understanding and clearer perception of His teaching, come to be regarded as Jesus' closest companions. They, of all the disciples, had been chosen to witness the raising of Jairus' daughter, and doubtless on other unrecorded occasions Jesus had taken them as His special companions during nights of prayer. At the last, too, they were to be nearest to Him in the darkness of

---

At His transfiguration the disciples were granted a momentary glimpse of the future glory of Christ.

By CARL BLOCH

Gethsemane. So bidding the other disciples make their way to a village for the night, Jesus led Peter, James, and John into the hills.

The location of the mountain which Jesus ascended has been the subject of considerable conjecture. Some have thought that it was one of the southern spurs of Mount Hermon, but the fact that they had already journeyed some considerable way would seem to preclude this. Moreover, when they met the disciples again the morning after, there was with them a large company of Jews, including some of the local rabbis, so that they must have left the more Gentile parts of northern Galilee behind.

A tradition which goes back to the early centuries of the Christian era identifies the mountain as Mount Tabor, a few miles south of the Sea of Galilee on the edge of the Plain of Esdraelon. So strong was this tradition that the ruins of no fewer than three churches are to be found on the table-like summit of the mountain. This identification is, however, as unlikely as the other, for the record expressly states that they did not "pass through Galilee" until the next day. It is also known, from the rock cisterns on the summit, that Tabor has always been an inhabited place, and in the days of Jesus a fortress crowned the hill. About A.D. 60, Josephus, governor of Galilee during the Jewish revolt, strengthened the walls in an endeavour to stem the advance of the Roman general, Vespasian, and the remains of his constructions are still to be seen. It is thus hardly likely that Jesus would have ascended Tabor in search of a quiet retreat for prayer.

We must, therefore, be content to leave unidentified the mountain where Jesus and His disciples spent the night, surmising that it was somewhere to the north of the Sea of Galilee, but not far removed from the Jewish cities beside the lake.

Jesus and His disciples had been walking all day and by the time they reached the top of the mountain in the gathering darkness, they were all weary. The three joined Jesus in their evening devotions and then, wrapping themselves in their cloaks, they lay down on the grass. As it was summer they needed no protection from the elements and were soon fast asleep.

Jesus, however, remained awake and, moving a little way from the sleeping group, began to pray earnestly. First, He prayed for strength to tread the path of suffering which lay darkly before Him to the cross. Then He prayed, that, for a brief moment, there might be unveiled before the eyes of His three chosen disciples the glory He had had with His Father from eternity in the past and which would be His again when His mission was completed.

God accepted His self-dedication and answered His prayer. As Jesus rose from His knees the veil of humanity, which He took upon Himself when He came to tabernacle with men, was drawn aside and the glory of the eternal Son shone through. The darkness of the night was dispelled by a celestial brightness which irradiated and transfigured the form of the Son of man.

The dazzling splendour awakened the disciples and when their eyes became accustomed to the unwonted brightness they looked up in wonder at the radiant form of Jesus. From the descriptions given to them by the three disciples, Matthew records that His appearance was as the sun, Mark compares it to snow in its purity and white-ness, while Luke declares that the appearance of Jesus was like lightning. Even His garments glowed and glistened.

Striking indeed is the similarity between the description of the transfigured Jesus and the inspired portrayals of Christ by Daniel and John. But whereas they recorded only visions of Christ's glory, the three disciples on the Mount of Transfiguration actually saw the glorified Jesus in person, for it is specifically stated that the disciples awoke to behold Him. They were not in a trance. It was not a dream. They did not see a vision. It was the Jesus they knew transfigured by the heavenly effulgence.

At His incarnation Jesus had "emptied Himself" of His glory; the divine Son was veiled in human flesh. In the transfiguration the veil was taken away. Jesus was freed from His human limitations and the glory of the divine Son flashed through. It was the miracle of the Incarnation in reverse.

If ever the disciples had doubted whether Jesus was "He that should come," they could not doubt it now. Here was visible confirmation of what Peter had declared by faith, that Jesus was the Son of the living God.

No wonder that years later this apostle, in one of his letters to the churches, confidently declared that he had not deceived them with "cunningly devised fables" about Jesus, for he and his fellow disciples had been "eye-witnesses of His majesty."

No wonder that John, who was with Peter on "the holy mount," declared in the opening verses of his gospel, "We beheld His glory, the glory as of the only begotten of the Father."

And if James, the third witness of the transfiguration, had not been the first of the apostles to "taste death" in the cause of Christ, doubtless he would also have recorded his abiding memory of that wonderful sight.

As the disciples gazed enraptured at the form of Jesus, they discerned two other figures of glorious appearance, one on either side, and engaging Him in earnest conversation. As they listened they heard the names of His companions. They were Moses and Elijah.

The presence of these two Old Testament worthies on this momentous occasion is taken by some to be a proof of the conscious existence of all the righteous dead. This conclusion, however, is quite erroneous. The Bible consistently teaches that the saintly dead are not yet in heaven, neither are the wicked dead in purgatory or any fiery hell. The Scriptures clearly reveal that the dead are "asleep," unconscious in the grave until the day Jesus returns, save for certain exceptional individuals, who, in the providence of God, have been permitted already to enter the glorious estate of heaven. Among these are Moses and Elijah.

Elijah, like one other Old Testament saint, Enoch, never died. Enoch walked with God so perfectly that the day came when he was "translated" without seeing death. He "was not; for God took Him." Elijah likewise was caught up in a "chariot of fire" to the heavenly realm without dying.

Moses did die, and was buried by God Himself in the mountains on the other

side of Jordan, but from this unknown grave he was called forth in a special resurrection as recorded in the epistle of Jude.

As a result of these unique circumstances, Moses and Elijah had already entered upon their heavenly service and could be commissioned by God to join Christ on the Mount of Transfiguration.

There were significant reasons for this divine commission. Moses was the instrument through whom God communicated the wonderful details of the sanctuary service, which vividly depicted the vicarious sacrifice of Christ, while Elijah was the greatest of the prophets who had proclaimed the coming of Messiah in glory. Elijah is also associated, in the last book of the Old Testament, with the warning message which was to herald Christ's second advent. "Behold," declared God through Malachi, "I will send you Elijah the prophet before the coming of the great and dreadful day of the Lord." John the Baptist announced the first advent of Christ in the "spirit and power of Elias" and the message of mercy and warning which precedes His second coming again is often called the "Elijah message."

Who then could more appropriately come to Christ on the threshold of the completion of His earthly life than these two, whose witness was to be fulfilled in Him? If the angels "desired" above all things to "look into" the mystery of divine love in human redemption, how much more would Moses and Elijah be anxious to talk with Jesus concerning His atoning sacrifice.

Certainly no more fitting embassy could have come from heaven to bring Jesus the token of His acceptance with His Father and an assurance of the efficacy of His vicarious death.

The Bible uses a remarkable word for the subject of the conversation between Moses and Elijah and Jesus. While in our version it is rendered His "decease," it is really His "departure" or "exodus." The death of Jesus was not like the death of any other human being. Life was not taken from Him as it is from man. Jesus voluntarily departed out of life and accepted death on behalf of man. He willingly took "the wages of sin" in order to free man from death's grip. Of His own will He entered the "gates of hell" in order to open up a way through resurrection to new life for His redeemed. And who could better encourage Him in His predestined task than Moses and Elijah, for whom death was already conquered?

Peter was first to find words in the presence of the ineffable glory. "It is good for us to be here," he cried in ecstasy. It was indeed, for what had been faith until that moment suddenly became sight in the unveiled glory of the Christ. So thrilling an experience was it that Peter wanted to forget the sad world below and stay for ever in the glory of the mount.

Quickly he went on addressing Jesus: "Let us make three tabernacles; one for

When Jesus returns the second time it will not be as a humble Babe, but in power and majesty.
By C. S. DIXON

Thee, and one for Moses, and one for Elias." It may be that, as the Feast of Tabernacles was not far away, he thought they could celebrate it there, but with his usual impetuosity, he did not consider what he was saying. For what he suggested could not be.

Jesus intended that the disciples should be strengthened by this foretaste of His triumph, but there was still work on earth for Himself and for them. He had to suffer and die and be raised from the dead. They had to go forth to proclaim a Christ crucified, risen, and coming again, that all might have the opportunity of sharing His glory. Only then could they be "for ever" with their victorious Lord.

Jesus did not reply to Peter in word, but he received his answer as a luminous cloud of glory came down and blotted out the wondrous scene. As the disciples stood paralyzed with fear, the voice of God spoke out of the cloud, "This is My beloved Son, in whom I am well pleased; hear ye Him."

To Jesus the words were an assurance that God was "pleased" with the way in which He had carried out His earthly task.

To the disciples they were an added testimony to the identity of Jesus as Peter later wrote, "For He received from the Father honour and glory, when there came such a voice to Him from the excellent glory, This is My beloved Son, in whom I am well pleased. And this voice which came from heaven we heard, when we were with Him in the holy mount."

Falling upon their faces before the presence of God the disciples dared not lift their heads for fear until the voice of Jesus bade them gently, "Arise and be not afraid."

When they took their hands from their eyes the glory had faded, the heavenly visitors had vanished. Only the familiar figure of Jesus stood before them. They were disappointed that the blissful experience had so soon passed away, but nothing could eclipse the assurance those moments brought to them. Gladly they would follow wheresoever He should lead.

By this time it was almost dawn and as the first light broke over the hills they descended the mountain track. As they walked Jesus counselled His disciples to say nothing of the events of the previous night "until the Son of man be risen again from the dead." They were not even to tell the other disciples. This command, strange as it may seem at first, underlines the purpose of the transfiguration. If the disciples had recounted their experience while Jesus was yet alive, they would not have been believed. The seemingly fantastic claim would only have exasperated the rulers of the Jews and increased their opposition to Him.

After the resurrection, however, it provided corroborative evidence of the miracle. The grave could not hold Him because He was the incarnate Son of God. And Peter and the other apostles effectively used the dramatic event of the transfiguration in their proclamation of the risen and glorified Son of God.

But the transfiguration was more than a witness that the Son of man was truly the Son of God; it was more than a manifestation of the heavenly glory He had set aside. It was also a preview of the future triumph of Christ at His second coming for His people.

Jesus had told His disciples at Cæsarea Philippi that some of them would "not taste of death" till they saw the Son of man "coming in His kingdom," and Peter, referring to the transfiguration in his second epistle testifies that it proclaimed not only the "power" but also the "coming of our Lord Jesus Christ."

The transfiguration was, in fact, a perfect miniature of His second coming.

In that glorious day Jesus will appear no longer in the "form of a servant," but in all His majesty as the divine King. "Then shall appear the sign of the Son of man in heaven," declared Jesus on a later occasion, "and they shall see the Son of man coming in the clouds of heaven with power and great glory."

The two companions of Jesus in His transfiguration similarly portray in miniature the two classes of people who will be "with Him" in the day of His triumph.

Moses, who died on Mount Nebo and was raised by God, represents the "dead in Christ" who will "rise" to be gathered by the angels into the presence of Christ. Moses' garb of glory likewise fittingly portrays the "body from heaven" with which they will rise and the "white raiment" of righteousness with which they will be clothed.

Elijah, on the other hand, because he was caught up to God without seeing death, represents the living righteous who will be transfigured into the likeness of Christ at His coming.

Moses and Elijah witness also to the reality of the life of the redeemed. Identity will be preserved, recognition will be mutual, while all mental and physical disabilities will have vanished in the glory of the eternal world.

In only one respect the transfiguration could not portray the final triumph of Christ and His people. The transfiguration was the experience of a moment, a transient preview of the coming glory, but when "the dead in Christ" rise and the living which "remain" are "caught up together with them in the clouds to meet the Lord in the air," the redeemed will not need, as Peter did, to beg to remain with Him in glory. They will be "ever with the Lord."

This chapter is based on Matthew 17:1-13; Mark 9:2-13; Luke 9:28-36.

Printed and published in Great Britain by The Stanborough Press Ltd., Watford, Herts.

SOUTHERN PALESTINE
in
BIBLE TIMES

Plain of Sharon

S A M A R I

● JOPPA

● LYDDA

● EMMAUS

AIN KAREM

● AZOTUS

● ASHKELON

J U D E A

● HEBR

● GAZA